Andrew,

with best wishes,

[signature]

September 2000

Change, Chance, and Optimality

Change, Chance, and Optimality

APRIL McMAHON

OXFORD
UNIVERSITY PRESS

OXFORD
UNIVERSITY PRESS

Great Clarendon Street, Oxford OX2 6DP

Oxford University Press is a department of the University of Oxford.
It furthers the University's objective of excellence in research, scholarship,
and education by publishing worldwide in

Oxford New York

Athens Auckland Bangkok Bogotá Buenos Aires Calcutta
Cape Town Chennai Dar es Salaam Delhi Florence Hong Kong Istanbul
Karachi Kuala Lumpur Madrid Melbourne Mexico City Mumbai
Nairobi Paris São Paulo Singapore Taipei Tokyo Toronto Warsaw

with associated companies in Berlin Ibadan

Oxford is a registered trade mark of Oxford University Press
in the UK and in certain other countries

Published in the United States
by Oxford University Press Inc., New York

British Library Cataloguing in Publication Data

Data available

Library of Congress Cataloging in Publication Data

Data applied for

ISBN 0–19–824124–0
ISBN 0–19–824125–9 (pbk)

1 3 5 7 9 10 8 6 4 2

Typeset in Minion
by Newgen Imaging Systems (P) Ltd., Chennai, India
Printed in Great Britain
on acid-free paper by
TJ International, Padstow, Cornwall

For Flora, who arrived in Chapter 3

Preface

Optimality Theory, which has developed and spread at speed through 1990s linguistics, is a good illustration of the fact that new theories are exciting, if not intoxicating. So many analyses of so many phonological phenomena have been presented in constraint-based terms that sheer volume is almost becoming an argument for OT in itself. To accept the theory, however, we really need to confront its basis as well as its results, and this requirement has shaped my own evaluation in two ways. First, I do not attempt to be comprehensive in my consideration of OT analyses: there is such a flood of these (and so many are available only electronically, where they may not be subject to the usual requirements of peer review; although it is pleasing to see more OT papers appearing now in more conventional journals), that the task would be never-ending, and runs the risk of becoming bogged down in detail. Secondly, my own interests in historical linguistics and evolutionary theory lead me to consider OT from the perspectives of sound change and the evolution of language, on the grounds that confronting theories with different types of data, and examining them from sometimes unexpected angles, can help us understand what they can do, and just as importantly, what they cannot and should not do.

I would like to thank the Humanities Research Board of the British Academy, as it then was, for the award of a period of research leave, during which I was able to start contemplating this project. I am grateful to audiences for comments and feedback on papers exploring some of the themes developed here, presented at the Second International Conference on the Evolution of Language in London; Current Trends in Phonology II in Paris; the tenth International Conference on English Historical Linguistics in Manchester; meetings of the Linguistics Association of Great Britain in Luton and Manchester; and at the Universities of

Cambridge, Oxford, Edinburgh and Durham: special thanks here go to Ricardo Bermúdez-Otero, Roger Lass, and Peter Matthews. Three readers for OUP supplied thoughtful and interesting comments, and improved the book very considerably, and John Davey, my editor at OUP, has been unfailingly helpful and supportive. Most of all, I thank my family: Rob, who continues to make it all possible, only in part by acting as translator and interpreter extraordinaire of the literature on genetics and evolution; and Aidan and Fergus, whose current daily struggles up the foothills of English remind me constantly how vital language is, and how important it is that we understand it.

AMSM

Cambridge, January 2000

Contents

1

Optimality Theory: the Basics

1.1 Past

If the health of an academic discipline is measured in terms of the liveliness of its controversies, then current phonological theory is clearly in good shape. Perhaps the most contentious area at present involves the formal objects of which a phonological model may be composed: specifically, we have a debate over rules and constraints.

In traditional generative models, following from Chomsky and Halle (1968), the basic tool of analysis is the phonological rule. Phonologists write a rule in response to some aspect of phonological behaviour in a particular language, or indeed dialect; thus, in German, the instruction 'devoice word-final stops' would account for the well-known alternation between [d] and [t] or [b] and [p]. This rule is given in a slightly more formal version in example (1.1.) below: note that nothing hangs on the particular formalism adopted, which is extremely old-fashioned in theoretical terms, but will suffice for exemplification.

(1.1.) German final devoicing:

$$\begin{bmatrix} + \text{ obstruent} \\ + \text{ voice} \end{bmatrix} \rightarrow [- \text{ voice}] \ /\text{- - -} \#$$

This rule describes the fact that, as (1.2.) shows, both voiced and voiceless stops are allowable word-initially and medially, while only the voiceless variety can appear at the ends of words.

(1.2.) *Tier* [tiːr] 'animal'   vs.   *dir* [diːr] 'to you'

   leiten [laitən] 'lead'   vs.   *leiden* [laidən] 'suffer'

BUT *Rat* [rat]   *Rates* [ratəs] 'advice'

   Rad [rat]   *Rades* [radəs] 'wheel'

   These distributional facts also determine the way the rule is written: the shape of an alternating form like *Rad* might seem to be equally accurately described by positing medial voicing, but this would leave non-alternating forms with voiceless medial stops, like *Rates* and *leiten*, as apparent exceptions. Since the point of the exercise is to make the rule generally applicable, rather than contradicted on the surface by data which do not conform to its predictions, it follows that we should write it as final devoicing.

   The form of phonological rules, then, is not random: but rules are by their nature language-specific, descriptive tools. Consequently, they are not directly explanatory: that is, they answer the 'what' question, and not the 'why' question. To progress beyond the descriptive level, generative phonologists have to call on expertise from other areas inside and outwith linguistics, and frame a response in terms of history; phonetics (which may, at a deeper level, mean physics or biology); memory; or acquisition, for instance. If rules are recognized as purely descriptive in this way, we also have a useful limit on their application: if a rule is proposed in the absence of appropriate surface behaviour for it to describe, then something is wrong. This sort of over-abstractness was common during the worst excesses of Standard Generative Phonology. Rules might be allowed to give 'free rides' to non-alternating forms (as was notoriously the case with Chomsky and Halle's (1968) Vowel Shift Rule, unwarrantedly extended from alternating pairs like *divine* ~ *divinity* or *crime* ~ *criminal* to *pine, swine* and *lime*); 'lay-by' rules removed apparently eligible forms temporarily from the scope of other processes; and underlying forms often contained non-surfacing elements (like an extraneous /x/ in *nightingale*), which would have to be removed or transformed by yet further rules.

One response to such overuse of rules, which constitutes a major trend in recent derivational phonology, is to propose constraints on their application, and thus, indirectly, on the abstractness of underlying representations. For instance, free rides are effectively outlawed by the Derived Environment Condition (earlier the Strict Cycle Condition) of Lexical Phonology (Kiparsky 1982; Hargus and Kaisse 1993), which permits a rule to apply only if its structural description is supplied by a preceding rule or the addition of a suffix, for instance. In the case of Trisyllabic Laxing in English, which provided Kiparsky's original illustration of Derived Environment effects, the rule applies in *divinity* because the addition of *-ity* makes originally disyllabic *divine* into a derived, extended form where the stressed *i* vowel falls three syllables from the end of the word, and therefore comes within the remit of Laxing. However, a form like *ivory*, which is underlyingly trisyllabic and has undergone no processes which might feed Trisyllabic Laxing, retains its tense initial vowel on the surface. This automatically entails less remote initial representations for non-alternating forms: *ivory* can be stored with an underlying initial vowel identical to the surface form, with no danger that this will be altered by an unconstrained Trisyllabic Laxing rule, while forms like *camera*, conversely, cannot be assigned underlyingly tense vowels in the first syllable and given a 'free ride' through Laxing. Hence, admittedly parochial rules do interact with universals in that they are answerable to our abilities and limitations as human beings; and this may include the restraining influence of presumably innate constraints like the Derived Environment Condition.

However, there are problems even for the most radically constrained version of rule-based, derivational phonology. First, although the rules are not intended as other than purely descriptive, and explanations are necessarily sought from outside phonology proper, phonologists have increasingly seen this as inadequate, because it is not possible, simply from looking at a rule, to see whether it is plausible or not. Word-final devoicing, as presented in (1.1.), looks almost identical to word-final voicing (1.3.); yet the former is very widely attested cross-linguistically and has a strong phonetic rationale, whereas the latter is bizarre at best.

(1.3.) Word-final voicing (highly unlikely):

$$\begin{bmatrix} + \text{ obstruent} \\ - \text{ voice} \end{bmatrix} \quad \rightarrow \quad [+ \text{ voice}] \quad / - - - \#$$

In a rule-based model, the rules and the underlying representations are also the focus of theoretical interest, and it is impossible to assign any real status to outputs, which are simply, and rather crudely, what we are left with when we run out of rules to apply in a particular case. Yet it is increasingly clear that outputs do play some controlling function in language, both diachronically and synchronically. For instance, in proportional analogy, language learners and users may produce inappropriate but rational surface forms essentially by copying the characteristics of other, similar surface forms (like *bring ~ brang ~ brung* by analogy with *sing ~ sang ~ sung*). It might be possible to see such effects as arising from extension of rules where they involve productive patterns, but many do not. Rule conspiracies, where a number of processes seem to interact to produce or prevent certain surface patterns, cause similar problems. For instance, in Yawelmani (Kenstowicz and Kisseberth 1979) we might propose the two rules in (1.4.).

(1.4.) Yawelmani:

a. Vowel deletion: $\begin{bmatrix} V \\ -\text{long} \end{bmatrix} \rightarrow \emptyset \quad / \quad VC - - - - CV$

b. Vowel insertion: $\emptyset \quad \rightarrow \quad V \quad / \quad C - - - - C \begin{Bmatrix} \# \\ C \end{Bmatrix}$

These rules, on the face of it, have opposite effects, with one removing structure and the other introducing it, so that they cannot be collapsed together into a single schema, as would be necessary in Standard Generative Phonology to show they are formally related. However, this is missing the generalization that these rules appear to conspire to produce CCV structures, but disallow *CC# and *CCC: both seem to be motivated, or driven, by the surface phonotactics of Yawelmani.

Finally, the role of constraints in rule-based generative phonologies is itself potentially unconstrained: we find a complex interaction of constraints with language-specific rules and properties. As (1.5.) shows, some constraints restrict rule applications in various ways, as discussed above for the Derived Environment Condition; but there are also constraints determining the permissible underlying representations for Language X, the permissible combinations of morphemes, and the permissible surface realizations. There is consequently a potential excess of theoretical machinery, and the possibility of deriving the same effects in various different ways, without any clear way of determining which is preferable.

(1.5.) Generative Phonology before OT (Archangeli 1997: 26):

      constraints hold here ⇒   underlying representation

                                    ⇓

      constraints hold here ⇒   morpheme concatenation

                                    ⇓

      constraints hold here ⇒   rules

                                    ⇓

      constraints hold here ⇒   surface representation

1.2 Present

Optimality Theory, which according to Archangeli (1997: 1) is '...THE Linguistic Theory of the 1990s', adopts a radically different approach: it focuses on limitations on natural language variability, and thus on constraining possible surface representations rather than rules. Indeed, in what we might call standard versions of Optimality Theory (Prince and Smolensky 1993), rules are excluded from the phonology in favour of constraints, and formal superiority is therefore claimed for OT since only a single type of formal object is involved: rules plus constraints give way to constraints alone. Since there are no rules and therefore no derivations, there is also no question as to the scope of the constraints, which will necessarily refer to outputs, simplifying the picture from (1.5.) considerably.

Furthermore, Optimality Theoretic constraints are not learned, as rules would have to be in a derivational model, but are 'given' as part of innate Universal Grammar; they are consequently universal. Explanation in OT also seems intended to be theory-internal: whereas a phonological rule is a descriptive response to language-specific behaviour, and requires explanation as a further, and typically external, step, in OT, phonological behaviour in any language is a response to the universal constraints and is in turn explained by them. The occurrence of final [t], [p] but not *[d], *[b] in German therefore reflects a universal, innate constraint disallowing final voiced stops. However, languages manifest behaviour which violates the constraints as well as phenomena which conform to their requirements, so that constraints are crucially defeasible; their effects are discernible from surface forms only if there is no higher-ranking, conflicting constraint. If there is, its satisfaction will be more important for the language in question than the violation of the lower-ranking constraint. Cross-linguistic differences, like the fact that English allows final voiced stops while German does not, therefore follow from constraint ranking, which is assumed to be learned: while the relevant constraint in German ranks fairly high, in English it must be outranked by some other constraint(s), which force its violation. Considering all possible outputs from all possible rankings of the constraints produces what is known as the factorial typology: only systems arising from some ranking or rankings will be possible human languages, while no impossible language should be derivable from any ranking.

However, although the OT constraints are formulated in response to outputs, their role in the theory is slightly more complex. In a rule-based derivational model, a single input for each (non-suppletive) morpheme is passed through the list of rules formulated for that particular language, to produce the appropriate output, or outputs, if alternation is involved. There are consequently a number of sequential steps and the derivation is a serial one. In OT, again, each output corresponds to a particular input form, but the constraints do not evaluate that input directly. Instead, the list of constraints, ranked appropriately for the language in question, evaluates a set of possible output candidates, as produced by 'a generation function GEN whose input is an underlying form and whose output is an infinite set of candidate forms derived from the input by unrestricted phonological operations' (Anttila 1997: 45). From this 'large space of candidate analyses' (Prince and Smolensky 1993: 5), the constraint system identifies the preferred output by a parallel process of harmonic evaluation, EVAL. That is, all the candidate parses are simultaneously compared against the appropriately ranked constraint list to see which violates fewest; or more accurately, which violates fewest higher-ranking constraints.

This process of evaluation is displayed on a constraint tableau like the one in (1.6.), which sets out how each candidate fares with each constraint. The unique winning representation is known as the maximally harmonic analysis.

(1.6.) Constraint tableau for /iu/ (after Sherrard (1997: 44–5)):

/iu/	*M/i	ONSET	NO COMPLEX NUCLEUS	*M/u
☞ a. iw		*		*
b. ju	*!			
c. i.u			**!	
d. .iu		*	*!	

In tableaux, solid vertical lines separate constraints crucially ranked with respect to one another, while dotted lines indicate ranking of these constraints is irrelevant, or cannot be ascertained from the data in question. Higher-ranking constraints appear further left. A constraint violation incurred by some representation is indicated by *, with ! marking the violation fatal to that parse. In (1.6.), the constraints *M/i and *M/u state that the high vowels are not permitted in syllable margins; that is, these vowels are preferentially nuclear. ONSET requires syllables to have an onset; and NO COMPLEX NUCLEUS permits only a single nuclear segment. Ranking of the constraints is determined by the recorded outcome: in other words, we know that *M/i outranks *M/u because the attested surface form in this hypothetical data set is [iw] (shown by the pointing hand in the tableau), and not [ju]. In a language with the opposite outcome (as suggested by English *you*, for example), the reverse ranking of the two constraints would be indicated.

To summarize, 'The constraints provided by Universal Grammar are simple and general; interlinguistic differences arise from the permutations of constraint-ranking; typology is the study of the range of systems that reranking permits' (Prince and Smolensky 1993: 5). The differences between this system and a rule-based approach are listed in (1.7.).

(1.7.) Advantages of OT (Archangeli 1997: 27):

1. It defines a clear and limited role for constraints.
   a. Each constraint is universal.
   b. Constraints are ranked in EVAL.

2. It eliminates the rule component entirely.
   Different constraint rankings ... express language variability.

3. It focuses research directly on language universals.
   Each constraint is universal.

4. It resolves the 'nonuniversality of universals' problem.
   Universals don't play the same role in every language.

1.3 Future?

It would appear, then, that Optimality Theory can unify the universal and language-specific aspects of phonology in a direct and explanatory way, and that it represents progress from its unsatisfactory rule-based precursor. Russell (1997: 110) makes this point very clearly: in derivational phonology, he says,

... the band-aids that were applied, such as enriched representations and principled general constraints, were needed so consistently in the same places that it raised suspicions over whether the ideas of phonological rewrite rules and sequential derivations might not be the fundamental problems. One might view Optimality Theory as the band-aids getting together, realizing their own power, and deciding that they could get along quite nicely without the patient.

In other words, just the general, universal constraints will suffice to cover the whole range of actual, language-specific data, without arbitrary and parochial phonological rules, which might in turn need to be constrained.

In the following chapters, however, I shall show that there are challenges to this view from various directions. First, to answer metaphor with metaphor, the thought of the band-aids managing without the patient (like the lunatics taking over the asylum) is not necessarily all that attractive. Concentrating on the technology can mean that the human aspects of a problem get lost. In linguistic terms, the interests, abilities and limitations of speakers, hearers and learners may lead to particular language-specific developments, and not all of these are reconcilable with a deeply universalist model like OT. Developing the theme, seeing Russell's band-aids as the focus, rather than the patient, may lead to an obsession with improving, refining and adding to the technology involved, without considering fully what its uses and limitations might be in the real world. A rudimentary tool like a scalpel (even a blunt and rusty one) in the right, skilled hands can perform a necessary operation; a finely honed, complex laser might in theory have more potential, but without the right instructions, properly assimilated, and the appropriate safety procedures, rigorously implemented, it is likely to do more harm than good. Again, we shall find in Chapters 2 and 3 that much current work in OT is devoted to simply proposing new constraints, many of dubious universality, and new mechanisms of constraint interaction. Yet none of this will be truly explanatory unless the constraints themselves are controlled and restricted: as Haspelmath (1999) puts it, we cannot hope to understand why ONSET and NOCODA, as opposed to NOONSET and CODA, are so frequently proposed in the OT literature, and why these match our intuitions about likely language patterns, if we do not know in principle why the constraints have the shape they have, and if we place no limits on the constraint set itself.

In short, I shall argue that OT, in attempting to confront the universal component of phonological behaviour, is in danger of failing to cope with the language-specific part. The focus of the theory is very clearly on these universal aspects: the first sentence of Kager (1999) tells us unequivocally that 'The central goal of linguistic theory is to shed light on the core of grammatical principles that is common to all languages.' Deriving language-specific variation and deviation from constraint interaction alone will only work, however, if all constraints are indeed universal: and in Chapter 2, I consider evidence that many allegedly universal constraints are effectively language-specific, and that OT cannot in fact function without the addition of parochial rules, or mechanisms which in some way mimic the operations found in traditional derivational models. My arguments and illustrations here and throughout will come from phonology and aspects of phonology–morphology interaction: OT is being extended to syntax (see Pesetsky 1997; Speas 1997; Grimshaw 1997; Kager 1999, Ch. 8), but OT syntax is developing its own mechanisms and priorities, and a full consideration of these and comparison with the prior, phonological applications of the constraint-based approach is beyond the scope of this book.

Much system-specific phonological behaviour follows from the history of the system concerned, and in Chapter 3 I outline the difficulties OT faces in accounting for sound change and its residue, as well as linguistic variation. In Chapter 4, I introduce comparisons with Natural Morphology and evolutionary biology, to show that the necessity of distinguishing system-specific from genuinely universal constraints extends well beyond phonology. Chapter 5 pursues the idea of evolution more directly: I argue that proponents of a strongly innatist approach like OT must consider how and why the allegedly universal constraints could have developed in our species. Throughout, we shall encounter many cases where, contrary to the Panglossian epigraph to Prince and Smolensky (1993), things could indeed be other than as they are: and finally, in Chapter 6, we return to Voltaire, in the light of experience, to consider Candide's uncomfortable question: ' "If this is the best of all possible worlds, then what must the others be like?" '

Optimality Theory may well be ' ... THE Linguistic Theory of the 1990s' (Archangeli 1997: 1): it remains to be seen how definitively the new millennium puts OT into the past tense.

2

Optimality in a Complex World: Additions and Extensions

2.1 The whole story?

Kager (1999: 187) sums up the arguments for Optimality Theory from the previous chapter in his claim that OT is 'conceptually superior', on the basis that his account of syncope in Southeastern Tepehuan, for instance, requires only constraints, whereas a classical derivational analysis would also need rules. That is, 'we find that a rule-based analysis uses excessive machinery to achieve effects that an OT analysis attributes to a single interaction' (Kager 1999: 188). Of course, if it were really a question of 'excessive machinery' on the one hand and straightforward ranking and *the* evaluation involving straightforward constraints on the other, there would be no contest. And indeed, there are some phonological phenomena which seem amenable to OT analysis in just this way; specifically, metrical and prosodic processes, including Kager's Southeastern Tepehuan case, fall regularly into this category. These are just the areas of phonology which were analysed, pre-OT, in a way most closely resembling OT: they often reflect cross-linguistic variation of small sets of units, with a restricted set of distributional options, and are relatively unaffected by complex morphophonological alternations.

However, there are other aspects of phonology which are describable perfectly adequately in rule-based, derivational terms, but where OT faces greater challenges. When we confront interactions of morphology with phonology; alternation; opacity;

language-specific processes with no clear universal rationale; and, as we shall see in Chapter 3, variation and change, the early, conservative version of OT presented in Chapter 1 is no longer able to cope. Consequently, in a relatively short period of time, OT has been extended and altered substantially, so that the claim of conceptual superiority on formal grounds is no longer so easy to substantiate. In particular, the number and type of constraints has increased massively: as Blevins (1997: 229) observes, 'Optimality Theory is in its early stages, and yet hundreds of markedness constraints have been proposed to account for sound patterns of the world's languages.' The first question arising from this is whether all these constraints are really universal, violable and innate. On examining the literature, we find that although all constraints are avowedly equal, in practice it seems that some are more equal than others.

2.2   Inviolable constraints and principles of constraint interaction

In rule-based phonologies, as we have seen, there are both rules and constraints. Some constraints are filters or phonotactic requirements, and operate on representations; others, like the Derived Environment Condition or Elsewhere Condition, cover rule applications and interactions. In this latter case, we find the main formal apparatus of the theory, namely the rules, subject to controls on their operation. While the conditions on representations are now converted to OT constraints, there is reason to believe that a higher level of principles must also be assumed in OT: here again, the main formal apparatus of the theory, now the violable constraints, must be subject to controls on their application and interaction.

Prince and Smolensky (1993: 186) provide a definition of a possible grammar as 'the well-formedness constraints provided by Universal Phonology, interacting via a particular dominance hierarchy consistent with the dominance conditions imposed by Universal Phonology', suggesting that we must recognize a superordinate level of principles. For instance, Pulleyblank (1997: 68) argues that ' ... the faithfulness constraint that enforces identity for place features in obstruents is *universally* ranked above the corresponding faithfulness constraint for nasals ... That is, OT proposes two types of rankings, (i) those that vary from language to language, and (ii) those that are invariant across languages.' One might suggest that this case follows from Pāṇini's Theorem on Constraint-ranking (Prince and Smolensky 1993: 107–8), which governs the relative ranking of specific and general constraints, with effects akin to that of the Elsewhere Condition. Given Prince and Smolensky's ascription of dominance conditions to Universal Phonology, the theorem might be characterized as an innate metacondition; however, Prince and Smolensky (1993: 108) contend that it 'is merely a point of logic, but the Elsewhere Condition is thought of as a principle specific to UG, responsible for empirical results which could very well be otherwise.' It is impossible to say whether this means Pāṇini's Theorem is innate but not specific to UG, or not innate and therefore irrelevant to learners or users of OT phonology, but perhaps useful to phonologists seeking to replicate their grammars.

In general, these principles are more often alluded to than defined: Kager (1999: 18), for instance, tells us that 'Both constraints and the general principles of their interaction are universal ... ', but does not expand on the nature of the principles themselves. Sometimes, results which are necessary to the operation of some part of the OT programme are simply stated as absolutes, and we are left to assume both that these are the result of some universal constraint on constraints, and what the nature of that condition might be: as we shall see in subsequent sections, this is true of Kager's contention that only ALIGN constraints can be language-specifically modified to include mention of specific morphemes, and McCarthy's assumption that the selector constraint in Sympathy theory must be an IO-Faithfulness constraint. Some absolute conditions seem more relevant to representations: thus, Bermúdez-Otero (1999) refers in his introductory list of conventions to 'Other grammatical statements, such as non-violable principles', and includes here Proper Headedness. This might be built into Gen as some sort of condition on inputs, but only at the cost of abandoning or significantly weakening the assumption of Richness of the Base, which requires that 'no constraints hold at the level of underlying forms' (Kager 1999: 19). Put slightly differently, all we need to know under Richness of the Base is that 'the input does not contain nonlinguistic objects' (Archangeli 1997: 13); formulating conditions on Gen as filters, or other input constraints, clearly complicates what we need to specify innately about the lexicon.

This last case leads us into a grey area between principles of constraint ranking and interaction on the one hand, and inviolable constraints, which might be stated, or referred to, as principles, on the other. There are certainly suggestions in the literature that certain constraints may be universally unviolated, including NUC (Prince and Smolensky 1993: 87), which requires all syllables to have a nucleus, and the related 'THM. Universally Optimal Syllables' (Prince and Smolensky 1993: 89), whereby no language may rule out .CV. syllables, and which consequently prevents languages from prohibiting onsets or requiring codas. OT constraints fall into two broad classes, namely markedness constraints, which relate to the structural well-formedness of outputs, and encode either positive requirements or negative prohibitions, and faithfulness constraints, which require identity (although see 2.4 below) between input and output forms: inviolable constraints will be of the markedness type, although of course not all markedness constraints will be inviolable, since some languages do have highly marked sounds in their inventories.

However, recognizing a specific class of undominated constraints would appear to conflict with Prince and Smolensky's (1993: 208) contention that 'Within Optimality Theory, all constraints have exactly the same status. The theory does not recognize, for example, a difference between "violable" and "inviolable" constraints.' Similarly, Kager (1999: 208) contends that a particular condition 'would not be a true OT constraint if it were unviolable.' In that case, the clustering of a certain set of constraints at the top of all dominance hierarchies, and the universal absence of violations of such constraints, will be fortuitous. In a discussion of the undominated constraint LX ≈ PR, which matches up phonological and morphological constituents, Prince and Smolensky argue that placing such constraints at the top of all possible hierarchies is not truly stipulative, since 'Any such condition fixes the range of relations between LX ≈ PR and many other constraints ... so the cost of the stipulation is amortized over a broad range of consequences ... ' (1993: 46). They continue (Prince and Smolensky 1993: 46, fn.26), 'More optimistically, we can expect to find principles of universal ranking that deal with whole *classes* of constraints.' In the current theory, however, there are no criteria for identifying such classes of constraints (since we saw above that the category of general principles has been little investigated), except perhaps in terms of relative ranking; and clustering together at the top of hierarchies is precisely the property we are seeking to explain. Either we must maintain Prince and Smolensky's (1993: 175) strong claim that 'all grammatical constraints are violable, in principle', or accept that certain constraints form a universally undominated class, characterized precisely by the property of inviolability, which then itself requires explanation, probably from outside phonology. That is, either we regard an undominated constraint requiring syllable nuclei and an empirically violable one requiring onsets as differing only in ranking, in which case the lack of exceptions to the former will remain fortuitous and there is no point in hypothesizing about ranking constraint classes, or we consider the inviolability of the former as important, and attempt to distinguish violable from inviolable constraints in terms of their *raisons d'être*, whereupon differential ranking might cease to be an issue. Of course, research on which constraints fall into the inviolable class, and therefore progress on any unifying factors, is unlikely to take place so long as OT denies the existence of inviolable constraints.

It seems odd that Prince and Smolensky should endorse the view that 'things cannot be otherwise' (*Candide*, Ch.1), without making the strong claim that there are constraints whose violation would take us outside the permitted range of natural language variation. Without such absolute constraints, Prince and Smolensky (1993: 175) themselves admit that ' ... it is not immediately obvious how the theory can account for the absolute impossibility of certain structures, either within a given language or universally.' Kager (1999: 105) contends that universally ungrammatical structures can always be ruled out simply by ranking violable constraints, since the factorial typology predicts that no possible ranking will deliver an impossible output. However, inviolable constraints may be necessary, as Archangeli (1997: 29) argues, if we are to understand the workings of Gen, since 'It is widely assumed that GEN can only create universally well-formed linguistic objects, that is ones which do not violate any universally inviolable constraints. This assumption requires that we distinguish between universally inviolable constraints and those which are violated, even if only rarely.' Without some such restriction, Gen will indeed produce the infinite set of forms from any input, since it would be able to add, remove or reorder any element; and as Archangeli (1997: 29) notes, 'Although this does not raise serious problems for formal research, it does hamper efforts to explore psycholinguistic and computational models of language, since neither responds happily to infinite sets.' Constraint evaluation of the conventional OT kind can only select the maximally harmonic parse; to dispose of candidates unequivocally, we need inviolable constraints like Orgun's (1996) Control set, which are actually able to mark an output as ungrammatical.

There is one further concern here, which relates to the innateness of constraints. Newmeyer (1998*b*) argues that the goal of grammatical theory should be to encode what is a possible human language, but not what is a probable one. That is, grammars do not incorporate typological generalizations, either directly or indirectly: typological considerations are therefore irrelevant to the construction or evaluation of grammars, and typological facts will require extragrammatical explanation. This kind of functional approach, to which we shall return in Chapter 3 in the context of sound change, tends to go along with a rejection of the assumption that OT constraints are innate (Hayes 1996; Haspelmath 1999). However, if there is a set of inviolable constraints, these might remain serious candidates for innateness, and a distinction of constraint types will therefore have considerable implications for the architecture of the theory, and perhaps particularly for acquisition under OT. In short, it may be true that '... for a given language, little tends to hang on whether a constraint undominated in that language is also inviolable universally' (Sherrard 1997: 47); but rather more may hang on this distinction for a theory fundamentally concerned with issues of universality.

2.3 System-specific strategies

2.3.1 Language-specific constraints

From inviolable constraints and possible metaconstraints, we descend to the other end of the dominance hierarchy, and to constraints which are of dubious universality. Sherrard (1997: 46) ascribes to OT a strong version of universality, whereby 'all constraints should be present in all grammars', but points out that 'In its full form, universality runs into problems of implementation: some constraints proposed in OT analyses appear so language-specific that it is hard to envisage them as being universally present in any useful sense.' Note that the problem here does not lie in the inclusion of language-specific devices in grammars *per se*: alternative, rule-based models, after all, contain virtually nothing else. The problem is including language-specific constraints while claiming that all constraints are universal and innate, or positing language-specific rules, as we shall see in 2.3.3 below, while claiming that OT uses only constraints.

Statements of the party line on universality in OT are not hard to find; but neither are acknowledgements that it is not strictly adhered to. Archangeli (1997: 15) notes that 'CON, as a universal set of constraints, is posited to be part of our innate knowledge of language. What this means is that every language makes use of the same set of constraints'—although of course, many will be ranked so low in the grammar of a particular language that they will have

no discernible effect, being uniformly outranked by other constraints. However, she continues (1997: 15 fn.3), 'The ideal which
Optimality research aims for (and sometimes appears to fall short
of) is to provide evidence of the universality of each constraint
necessary for some particular language ... there are numerous
analyses involving constraints whose status as a universal is minimal at best.' Similarly, Kager (1999: 11), again discussing universality, points out that 'In its strongest interpretation, by which all
constraints are part of UG, this implies that all constraints are
part of the grammars of all natural languages.' However, he
admits that 'This strong interpretation, which leaves no room for
language-specific constraints nor for constraint variability', must
be 'slightly relativized'.

The exceptions Kager discusses involve the interaction of morphology and phonology as encapsulated in ALIGN constraints, and
we turn to these in 2.5 below. However, there are many cases of
apparently language-specific constraints which do not fall directly
into this category. The contradiction between claiming universality
and maintaining it is already obvious in Prince and Smolensky
(1993), where constraints are permitted to vary on a language-
specific basis: hence, for instance, we find discussion of the best way
to 'formulate a satisfactory version of NONFINALITY for Latin'
(1993: 43). Although NONFINALITY is later reformulated in a
more general way, the option of parameterizing the constraint is
left open (Prince and Smolensky 1993: 52). Parametric variation is,
of course, a familiar concept, and language-specific modification of
only this circumscribed type might be relatively unobjectionable,
given some indication of the set of constraints which could vary in
this way. Other analyses, however, present greater problems. Most
notably, in their account of augmentation and truncation alternations in Lardil, which they argue to be prosodically driven, Prince
and Smolensky propose the constraint in (2.1.).

(2.1.) 'FREE-V.
        Word-final vowels must not be parsed (in the nominative).'
                                    (Prince and Smolensky 1993: 101)

This certainly covers the relevant segmental losses in Lardil, but the constraint is indubitably specific to that system. Prince and Smolensky (1993: 101) accept that 'Although FREE-V takes the bull by the horns, it would not perhaps be put forth as the canonical example of a universal markedness principle.' However, they continue to defend their general approach, arguing that:

Any theory must allow latitude for incursions of the idiosyncratic into grammar. What is important for our program is that such incursions are best expressed as *constraints*; that they are (slightly) modified versions of the universal conditions on phonological form out of which core grammar is constructed; and that they interact with other constraints in the manner prescribed by the general theory.

This statement is unclear for several reasons. First, we are not told which constraint FREE-V is a '(slightly) modified version' of: although Prince and Smolensky relate FREE-V to the prosodic weakness of final open syllables (1993: 101) and to extrametricality constraints (1993: 123), they do so only informally. The limit of the (slight) modification permitted is also unclear, as is the question of which constraints can be modified. For instance, it seems likely that at least those constraints found at the top of all dominance hierarchies are not subject to variation, suggesting again that a distinction should be made between absolutely inviolable constraints where any modification would create impermissible structure, and all others.

For some language-specific statements, it is hard even to identify a universal constraint to modify. Prince and Smolensky (1993: 103) refer, again in their account of Lardil, to 'constraints against geminate consonants and against the sequence řt.' These seem fairly cut-and-dried statements, and instead of parametric variation, Prince and Smolensky presumably envisage such constraints as ranking high in languages like Lardil, but low to the point of invisibility in languages where geminates or řt occur frequently. This implies that there are innate constraints referring to every possible segment or sequence type, and that the learner has to suppress these constraints during acquisition in rather the way assumed in Natural Generative Phonology, where children are seen as suspending natural rules which they are predisposed to apply, just in case these are not manifested in the relevant input data (Stampe 1972; Donegan 1993). In OT terms, presumably learners rank these constraints so low that no further reference need be made to them: we return to these issues of learnability, negative evidence and innateness in 2.7 below. However, the assumption that these *SEG constraints are innate is supported by other OT analyses. For instance, Ringen and Vago (1998: 398), in an account of Hungarian vowel harmony, propose the segmental markedness constraint *ɨʌ, 'Vowels which are [+back] and [−low] must be specified as ROUND': but their analysis also involves a much more extensive use of such markedness constraints for a wide range of segments, as shown in their claim that ' … the markedness constraints *ü, *ö and *ɛ are ranked above the constraints *u, *o and *ɔ/a, which will mean that the optimal outputs for the input root vowels U, O and A (i.e. vowels unspecified for backness) will be [u], [o] and [ɔ] (or [a:]) respectively' (Ringen and Vago 1998: 405). There are even more specific cases of such prescriptions: take, for instance, SHORT ɛ (Ringen and Vago 1998: 408), which requires that ' … if a vowel is short, front, non-high and unrounded it must be low, and if it is long, it must be mid.' If segmental and inventorial restrictions of this sort are to be handled for all languages (and all possible languages, since our knowledge is necessarily partial) using innate constraints, then it follows that the constraint list will be extremely long and its organization into language-specifically relevant versus irrelevant categories potentially a Herculean task of acquisition. That is, at the moment there remains a possibility of confusion between what is plausibly learnable on the basis of data from a single language, and what is universal, or at least ascribable to a universal principle or tendency.

Prince and Smolensky (1993: 104) themselves note, of the constraints proposed for Lardil, that 'only FREE-V involves a significant degree of language-particular idiosyncrasy', perhaps suggesting that they see such idiosyncrasy as unfortunate. This impression might be supported by the efforts Prince and Smolensky make to identify cross-linguistic congeners for the phenomena they identify wherever possible; thus, they (1993: 118) describe a particular syllable type as 'cross-linguistically attested ... and therefore suitable for being controlled by a rankable constraint.' In fact, there are many cases of such implicit or explicit apology in the OT literature when effectively language-specific constraints are proposed. We have already encountered the strategy of characterizing the language-specific constraint as a modification of a universal one, which may or may not be identified. Another option is to present constraints as preliminary: McCarthy (1998*b*: 5) proposes the rather Nootka-specific constraints shown in (2.2.) to handle alternations involving labialization and delabialization, but argues that 'The constraints themselves are universal; their interaction through ranking is language-particular and learned. Here I will focus on just the interaction, glossing over details of constraint formulation that are not relevant in this context.' Note also that these constraints are given names, albeit in scare quotes, which are rule-like and processual. Constraint (2.2.a) prohibits plain dorsals after rounded vowels, while (2.2.b) rules out syllable-final rounded dorsals.

(2.2.) Constraints for Nootka

    a. "ROUNDING"

        $*oK$

    b. "UNROUNDING"

        $*K^{w}]_{\sigma}$

                                    (McCarthy 1998*b*: 5, (8))

    Presenting apparently language-specific statements as constraints in progress is becoming a relatively common strategy: for instance, Lin (1997) proposes the constraint in (2.3.) for Piro.

(2.3.) '*CCC: Three-consonant clusters are prohibited. (*tentative*)'

Bermúdez-Otero (1999: 177) adopts precisely this marking of '(tentative)' for his novel constraint *i.j, which is necessary for his account of West Germanic Gemination (see 2.6 below). In all these cases, however, we are faced with additional, language-particular constraints which are presented as in need of revision, or at least of reassignment to some superordinate constraint; and this kind of strategy is only helpful if that revision is actually forthcoming. Public confession may indeed be good for the soul, and recognizing a problem is perhaps a partial step forward; but it is not the same as solving it.

2.3.2 The reintroduction of rules

A more radical option would be to recognize that language-specific statements are necessary in OT. McCarthy (1999) is quite right in his assertion that a theory like OT, in which one theoretical strength is the reduction of formal machinery, should reject any non-universal constraints on the basis of Occam's Razor: if language-specific ranking can give the right results, then the extra complexity of language-specific constraints simply is not required. However, McCarthy also notes that an Occam's Razor argument cannot trump an empirical one: the first says we should do without language-specific statements if possible, but there may be data which suggest this is not feasible after all. The evidence reviewed in the last section (along with further sound change data presented in Chapter 3) suggests strongly that this is the case.

If language-specific statements are required, the next question is what form they should take within OT. Language-specific constraints are one possibility; these will raise issues of innateness, for reasons reviewed in Chapter 5 below, and their interaction with universal constraints will also have to be clarified. On the other hand, parochial rules, outside the constraint system, have also been reintroduced in a number of OT analyses. Interestingly, these proposals typically involve non-prosodic, segmental areas of phonology, where OT seems impressionistically to work far less well. For instance, Prince and Smolensky (1993) deal with epenthesis and deletion, as long as these can be seen as prosodically motivated, and with phenomena like quantity adjustments and resyllabification; but their remit does not extend to the majority of traditionally defined morphophonemics. Thus, they consider the length distinction in English *keep ~ kept*, but not the vowel quality alternation (1993: 211); and in Lardil, they note that ' ... the ending *-uṛ* undergoes various morphophonemic modifications of limited or unclear generality which will not be dealt with here' (1993: 100). Even more tellingly, again in connection with Lardil, Prince and Smolensky (1993: 98) note:

There are a number of segmental and allomorphic alternations which will not be treated here, including the lowering of final vowels *u, i → a, e* and the process of sonorization t, ṭ → r, ɾ / --- #, of which the latter may be relevant to a later level of phonology than we discuss ... These can be safely abstracted away from inasmuch as they do not interact with basic syllabification, which lies at center of our concerns.

Even leaving aside the unexplained reference to 'a later level of phonology', the nature and scope of this disclaimer is unclear. It seems clear that Prince and Smolensky are setting aside these segmental alternations precisely because they are not prosodically conditioned; but this may reflect an intentional (and perhaps short-term) decision to concentrate OT on prosodically driven phonology, or an empirical discovery that prosodic phonology is all that OT is really suited to. It is possible that general constraints of the OT type are more relevant for certain areas of phonology than others, reflecting the existence of universal, finite categories and constituents in prosodic phonology, whereas matters of vowel and consonant quality reflect continua to a greater extent, are less directly ascribable to universal constraints, and perhaps more open to the disruptive effects of cumulative sound changes, even where such universals are ultimately at issue. This is not, of course, to say that OT would be any less valuable if it were discovered to be limited to prosodic phonology: on the contrary, as

Pesetsky (1997: 135) suggests in connection with the extension of OT from phonology to syntax,

It would be equally interesting ... if we were to learn ... that optimality-theoretic interactions characterize *some, but not all*, aspects of language. We would then face the intriguing task of discovering exactly what Optimality Theory is and is not good for—and, ultimately, under-standing the reasons for any divisions of labor that we may find.

For the moment, however, OT is clearly expanding beyond directly prosodically-conditioned phonology, and it is in these segmental areas that the greatest proliferation of constraints and the strongest tendency to accept parochial rules is to be found. One of the earliest suggestions that rules may be required in OT is found in McCarthy (1993), an OT account of linking and intrusive [r] in non-rhotic Eastern Massachusetts English. Linking [r] surfaces before a vowel as in *car engine*, but is absent before a pause or consonant, as in *car park*; intrusive [r], a relatively recent development found in *draw*[r]*ing, idea*[r] *is*, has a similar distribution in terms of context, but involves an extension of [r] beyond the set of lexical items in which it is etymologically appropriate. McCarthy initially derives intrusive [r] from the interaction of two constraints, given in (2.4.).

(2.4.)   CODA-COND   FINAL-C

        *VrX]σ   *V]PrWd

CODA-COND requires [r] to be in the syllable onset, while FINAL-C prohibits Prosodic Words from ending in a short vowel. Forms like *Wanda*[r] *arrived, Home*[r] *arrived* then obey FINAL-C; **Wanda*[r] *left* and **Home*[r] *left* are ruled out by CODA-COND; and since CODA-COND ranks higher, it forces the violation of FINAL-C in *Wanda left, Homer∅ left*.

McCarthy is left with the problem of specifying why [r] is the consonant intruded in *Wanda*[r] *arrived*. The Faithfulness constraints of OT, FILL and PARSE, govern empty slots and maintain

as close a correspondence as possible between initial and surface representations: we might then hypothesize an empty
consonantal slot □ in cases of intrusive [r], with CODA-COND
stated for □, since /r/ will be absent from initial representations.
However, such epentheses in OT typically involve default segments, and as McCarthy notes in the Appendix to his paper, '*r* is
demonstrably not the default consonant of English' (1993: 190).
Consequently, 'the output form *Wandar arrived* must differ seg-
mentally (melodically), rather than just prosodically, from the
corresponding input form /Wanda arrived/' (ibid.). Since
McCarthy sees melodic conservation as central in defining the
normal OT candidate set, he proposes broadening the candidate
set in this case by employing a phonological rule $\emptyset \rightarrow$ r. As he
explains (1993: 190),

By a "rule" here I mean a phonologically arbitrary stipulation, one that
is outside the system of Optimality. This rule is interpreted as defining
a candidate set {Wanda, Wandar}, and this candidate set is submitted to
the constraint hierarchy. That is, this rule enlarges the candidate set to
include non-melody-conserving candidates like *Wandar arrived* (and
*Wandar left), which are then evaluated by the constraint hierarchy in
the familiar way.

This rule is therefore necessary 'to enlarge the candidate set
in a very limited way, stipulating the phonologically unnatural
phenomenon of *r* epenthesis' (McCarthy 1993: 191). We shall
return to the details of McCarthy's analysis, and specifically to
the question of just how unnatural [r]-intrusion is, in Chapter 3:
for the moment, let us concentrate on more general aspects of
McCarthy's proposal to include parochial rules in OT.

Halle and Idsardi (1997: 337–8) clearly believe that McCarthy's
r-insertion rule has no place in OT, arguing that 'Conceptually,
reliance on an arbitrary stipulation that is outside the system of
Optimality is equivalent to giving up on the enterprise. Data that
cannot be dealt with by OT without recourse to rules are fatal
counterexamples to the OT research programme.' Equally, if constraints are crucially violable, and optimality is therefore relative,

it is difficult to see what can *be* outside the system. Even at best, it is certainly true that, to reconcile rules with OT, we would have to understand the part they are intended to play in the theory, and the circumstances in which they can acceptably be introduced. Thus, McCarthy's reference to a 'phonologically unnatural phenomenon' is circular if it simply refers to processes which cannot be analysed within OT as it stands, and we need some further, external definition of (un)naturalness. Perhaps more straightforwardly, we require an idea of how rules will interact, not only with the constraints of OT, but with its other major mechanism, namely Gen.

McCarthy seems to rule out melodic alteration via Gen, but this does not square with Roca's (1997: 3) statement that, while Gen 'provides the target form [AC] from the source [AB]', it 'also supplies a large (possibly infinite) number of competitors, among them [AB], [AD], [AF], [ABZ], [FGHIJK], etc.'. Similarly, Kager (1999: 20) suggests that Gen is subject to Freedom of Analysis, whereby 'any amount of structure may be posited'; in early versions of OT, Gen was restricted by the Principle of Containment, which required that the input should always be included in the output; but this has been abandoned under Correspondence Theory (see 2.4 below) so that Gen now effectively allows deletion, and in any case, Containment would not have banned insertion of structure by Gen. Consequently, there seems no good reason why Gen should not supply candidate forms with [r]. Paradis and LaCharité (1993: 139) also point out that Gen could equally well produce candidates like *spat* or *spaʔ* rather than *spar*, which conform to both CODA-COND and FINAL-C in McCarthy's analysis: why then do some maximally harmonic forms, that is, those which surface in English, have to violate either constraint at all? Paradis and LaCharité (1993: 148) conclude that ' ... the internal workings of GEN are largely unexplored', and that a conflict exists: on the one hand, we cannot constrain Gen too strictly, 'for without a rich candidate set to choose from, only extreme good fortune can account for the actual output'; on the other, if Gen is left to overgenerate freely, 'why must we ever settle for an output that violates a constraint when an infinite field of candidates would make available forms that conform to all the constraints?'

If Gen provides a large or even infinite candidate space for each input, and only one output is selectable, it follows that extreme overgeneration is intrinsic to OT; as Paradis and LaCharité (1993: 147) see it, 'this overgeneration ... is an extremely costly and unexplanatory device. It departs from previously accepted scientific criteria (economy, power of prediction, links between facts, etc.) which normally serve to evaluate the adequacy of a phonological analysis.' Gen may even produce such a large space of candidate analyses that those for any one form will also include those for any other, a situation which might even equate with storing a vast number of options not linked to any particular form. This extreme power of Gen has not been much discussed in the OT literature, perhaps because it is not evident from tableaux, which characteristically evaluate only a small, decidedly finite set of options (and typically the more sensible ones at that). Indeed, Blevins (1997: 234) points out that the dominant view of Gen as parallel provides 'no effective means of verifying tableaux. Current tableaux contain a designated optimal candidate along with several other candidates chosen essentially at random. We need to know not that the candidate is better than *some* other candidates, but rather that it is better than *all* other candidates.' This is reminiscent of the problems encountered by phylogenetic tree-drawing programs in biology, such as PAUP (Swofford 1990) and PHYLIP (Felsenstein 1989), which aim to ascertain the degree of relatedness among species by generating all possible trees for the data-points concerned, then identifying the best-fit tree. However, because the numbers being worked with are so absurdly huge, with 15 populations giving 2×10^{14} rooted trees, algorithms exist to write off large families of potential trees at an initial stage. Since it is always possible, albeit unlikely, that the true tree is in this batch of rejected trees which were never fully considered, the statistical technique of bootstrapping is employed to test the robustness of the best-fit tree, rerunning the analysis over many repetitions to see how frequently this tree, or something very like it, emerges. OT involves a similar overgeneration and selection of candidate analyses, but without either an algorithmic way of determining the parses ruled out *a priori* and never appearing in a tableau, or the bootstrapping test for robustness. The latter is arguably unnecessary: whereas in biology the tree drawing exercise is designed to find something out, where relations among species are not known or are uncertain, in OT the optimal parse is identified in advance by its surface occurrence in the language being described. The constraints then have to be manipulated in such a way as to ensure selection of this form. However, while this may make bootstrapping redundant (with Gen, in this light, seeming a rather sterile aspect of the theory), the absence of methods for deciding which candidates to consider is a more telling weakness.

This restriction of candidates in tableaux is typically presented as simply a space-saving device rather than a matter of theoretical significance: Archangeli (1997: 12) suggests, for instance, that 'Given that GEN creates an infinite set of candidates, a necessary strategy when presenting tableaux is to restrict the candidates presented in the tableau to those which are critical to the point being made—the infinite set could not possibly be considered!' This still leaves potential indeterminacy in the model, however; and unless we know how language users narrow down the candidates considered, we are left with the problem of infinity and the inevitable difficulties it raises for OT as a production or processing model. Kager (1999: 26) plays down this concern, arguing that 'Explaining the actual processing of linguistic knowledge by the human mind is not the goal of the formal theory of grammar.' A thought-experiment may decide our attitude to this claim: if Kager is right, and we one day find out how processing really operates, we should not care one way or the other whether its workings match our model. I rather think we would be pleased if we discovered it did.

Blevins (1997) proposes a unified response to the introduction of rules into OT and to the restriction of Gen. She suggests that 'phonological rules are language-specific generation strategies indexed to particular constraints. If a rule indexed constraint is violated, the phonological rule applies first, bleeding application of further Gen operations' (1997: 234). For intrusive [r], McCarthy's r-insertion rule will be indexed with FINAL-C, and constitutes a repair strategy triggered by violation of that constraint, the interaction between the two being determined by the Elsewhere Condition. For this proposal to work, however, Blevins must reject the parallel version of Gen preferred by Prince and Smolensky (1993) for an alternative serial–sequential model. It is clear that this interesting approach will circumscribe Gen, but various open questions remain. For instance, if Gen is to operate serially, a limit on the number of constraints proposed may be required, or the computation involved will quickly become excessive. Blevins also sees her approach as beneficial in that 'Instead of reverting to the position that some constraints are universal, while others are language-specific, one can remain agnostic on the universality of constraints by relegating all language-specific phonological rules to a specific generation block distinct from the constraint hierarchy' (1997: 234).

However, for this to be a satisfactory solution it is essential to have some means of determining what phonological behaviour should be ascribed to a rule, and what to a constraint. It is unclear whether constraints should take priority, with a rule proposed only if the constraint framework is unable to identify the appropriate candidate, as in McCarthy (1993), or whether we should seek criteria for distinguishing the two categories. Language-specificness alone does not seem a sufficient criterion, for two reasons. First, it will be extremely hard to quantify how much cross-linguistic data is necessary to invoke a constraint rather than a rule: to take a nonsense example, would a sound change creating in Welsh an alternation hitherto only known in Quechua justify suddenly replacing the Quechua rule with a universal (and innate) constraint? Second, Blevins herself seems to be operating with three categories, including language-specific constraints as well as universal constraints and rules. For instance, in her analysis of Gilbertese, she proposes various constraints on the syllable requiring codas to be nasal, and permitting only labials domain-medially in codas; and even more clearly, she notes that (1997: 239) 'a unique constraint in

Gilbertese demands that phrases (XP) constitute minimally trimoraic sequences,' while also proposing an actual phonological rule for Gilbertese nasal sandhi. Again, we face a lack of clarification, perhaps to be expected at this early stage but certainly in need of attention, on the distinction between constraints and rules in OT.

Blevins (1997) argues that phonological rules like r-insertion in English or Gilbertese nasal sandhi are reanalyses of originally phonetically motivated alternations, and that their productivity and frequent occurrence makes them straightforward to learn. However, she accepts that this will not be true of all language-specific phenomena. She considers the more opaque FREE-V in Lardil, for instance, to be a language-specific morphological rule, which is not ranked among the phonological constraints, but forms part of a morphological component providing inputs to the phonology. Prince and Smolensky, on the other hand, regard FREE-V as a modification of an extrametricality constraint, and attribute it to the weakness of final open syllables; however, Blevins (1997: 256) argues that this is true only 'in the most indirect sense', and that the loss of final vowels in the nominative in Lardil instead reflects the historical reinterpretation of final vowels as case markers, leading to a synchronic subtractive rule in the morphology. This separation of morphology and phonology seems likely to disallow interweaving constraints from different grammatical subsystems, potentially losing many insights of Lexical Phonology (unless, of course, the 'later level of phonology' mysteriously referred to by Prince and Smolensky (1993: 98) in fact includes interaction of some kind; and see 2.5 below). However, the envisaged separation of levels does not seem strict: recall Blevins's (1997: 239) 'unique constraint in Gilbertese' requiring 'that phrases (XP) constitute minimally trimoraic sequences', which must be a phonological constraint referring to syntactic constituents, or a syntactic one involving the (phonological) mora. Either way, the interaction between different areas of the grammar in OT requires further attention, as does the interaction among constraints, rules, and Gen.

2.4   Correspondence Theory

Although not all proponents of OT wish to include rules explicitly in their analyses, further mechanisms with much the same effects are being added. This is particularly true within Correspondence Theory, the current instantiation of Faithfulness. Prince and Smolensky (1993) maintained input–output proximity and, as we saw above, excluded deletion operations from Gen, by assuming the Principle of Containment, whereby the input must be contained in every output candidate. Input and output did not need to be identical, however; the degree of closeness depended on the ranking of the Faithfulness constraints FILL and PARSE, which prohibit epenthesis and deletion respectively. However, as usual, the requirements of a higher-ranking constraint might motivate, for instance, a PARSE violation: the resulting unparsed slot would be phonetically uninterpretable and hence unrealized, allowing for a percept of deletion and hence input–output disparity.

The replacement of Containment Theory by Freedom of Analysis (Kager 1999: 20, 100), whereby Gen is unrestricted, leads to Correspondence Theory (McCarthy and Prince 1995). Here, input and output need not, even in the ideal case, match precisely; instead, the revised Correspondence constraints control the extent of the match between input and output. The constraints DEP-IO and MAX-IO operate at the segmental level, and like FILL and PARSE, control epenthesis and deletion respectively. The new constraint IDENT-IO will determine whether input and output have the same value for some phonological feature; since this relation can be stated individually for each feature, IDENT-IO is really a group of constraints.

We shall return to MAX and DEP in Chapter 3, in the context of synchronic and historical epenthesis and deletion. However, Correspondence Theory has also spawned a significant number of other constraints and constraint types. Some of these involve relationships, not between the input and output, but between two output candidates, or between two morphologically related forms (see also 2.5 below); others relax the definition of correspondence in various ways. Most of these developments are attempts either to capture morphology–phonology interactions without recourse to level-ordering, or to deal with phonological opacity, which, as Kager (1999: 377) accepts, 'is OT's Achilles heel'.

In rule-based phonologies, rules may misapply, in that ' ... an alternation is triggered outside its proper environment, or it fails where all its conditioning requirements are met ... This counter-intuitive quirk of phonological grammars is called opacity' (Bermúdez-Otero 1999: 56). Counterintuitive though this may be, its existence is predicted in such derivational models, both by the existence and mode of interaction of rules themselves, and by the appearance in the derivation of intermediate levels of representation which are neither underlying nor surface forms, but arise artefactually from the application of some rule. These intermediate levels seem in certain cases to provide evidence for a puzzling surface form: that is, opaque generalizations become quite transparent if we can look at the stages in a serial derivation.

Kager (1999: 373) provides the example in (2.5.) from Turkish, where the processes of vowel epenthesis and velar deletion interact.

(2.5.) Vowel epenthesis in Turkish

    a. Vowel epenthesis

| /baʃ-m/ | [ba.ʃɨm] | 'my head' |
| /jel-m/ | [je-lim] | 'my wind' |

    b. Velar deletion

| /ɑjɑk-I/ | [ɑ.jɑ.ɨ] | 'his foot' |
| /inek-I/ | [i.ne.i] | 'his cow' |

    c. Interaction

| /ɑjɑk-m/ | [ɑ.jɑ.ɨm] | 'my foot' |
| /inek-m/ | [i.ne.im] | 'my cow' |

Forms like [ba.ʃɨm] show that word-final consonant clusters attract an epenthetic vowel, while cases like [ɑ.jɑ.ɨ] demonstrate the deletion of intervocalic /k/. Both processes have applied to give [ɑ.jɑ.ɨm], but only the context for velar deletion is apparent from the surface form: that is, velar deletion applies transparently, but vowel epenthesis is opaque here. To understand why vowel epenthesis has been allowed to apply, we require access to the representation preceding velar deletion: in different cases of opacity, this may be the underlying form, or an intermediate one.

In OT, which is output-oriented, the occurrence of opacity is not predicted. Kager (1999: 376) suggests the constraints in (2.6.) to capture the Turkish facts from (2.5.).

(2.6.) a. *VkV = no intervocalic [k]

   b. *COMPLEX = no consonant clusters

Since these constraints never conflict, their relative ranking cannot be determined; however, to get the right results for epenthesis and velar deletion individually, it is clear that both must outrank MAX-IO, which must in turn outrank DEP-IO. When these constraints are placed in a tableau, however, as shown in (2.7.), it is clear that the actual winning candidate cannot be selected by Eval: the most harmonic, transparent candidate, shown by the sad face, actually fails to surface.

(2.7.)

Input: /ajɑk-m/	*COMPLEX	*VkV	MAX-IO	DEP-IO
a. ɑ.jɑkm	*!	*		
b. ɑ.jɑ.kɨm		*!		*
c. ɑ.jɑ.ɨm			*	*!
d. ☹ ɑ.jɑm			*	

As Kager (1999: 377) observes, 'This finding destroys all hope that the problem is solvable without the help of additional

constraints (or even new theoretical machinery)', and these additions will be the subject of the next three sections.

First, Archangeli and Suzuki (1997) exploit the flexibility of
Correspondence Theory by introducing what Kager (1999: 381)
calls 'two-level well-formedness' in their analysis of (non-prosodic)
processes of lowering, raising and harmony in Yawelmani Yokuts.
There are two novel aspects to this account, both of which add considerably to the power of the theory: one feature in the input can
be placed in correspondence with a different feature in the output;
and reference to both input and output is accordingly extended
from faithfulness to well-formedness constraints, effectively neu-
tralizing the distinction between the two types.

Yokuts manifests a set of lowering alternations, whereby long
vowels surface as non-high, as shown in (2.8.): note that the suffix [-aaʔaa-] requires a short vowel in the preceding root.

(2.8.)

taan-it	'was gone'	tanaaʔaahin	'had gone'
meek'-it	'was swallowed'	mik'aaʔan	'is swallowing'
ʔooṭ'-ut	'was stolen'	ʔuṭ'aaʔaanit	'is going to be stolen'

Archangeli and Suzuki (1997: 203) argue that ' … if correspond-
ence-based OT is to account for the full pattern, then we must refer
to the correspondence of non-identical elements. That is, we consider faithfulness constraints to be only a subclass of the correspondence constraints.' Hence, they propose a disparate correspondence
constraint (2.9.), allowing non-identical elements to correspond:
here, input length corresponds to output non-highness.

(2.9.) Lowering: μμIℜO [−high]

'Any output correspondent of an input long vowel must be
[−high]'

                                        (Archangeli and Suzuki 1997: 203)

This, however, leads to another problem, since surface [e ee] will now be derived from input high vowels, but faithfulness will prefer initial /meek'-it/ to Archangeli and Suzuki's desired /miik'-it/ for surface [meek'-it] 'was swallowed'. The solution is an input markedness constraint (2.10.), which determines the shape of possible inputs, therefore conflicting with Richness of the Base. Kirchner (1997: 93) argues that constraints referring to features in the input only should be ruled out as unacceptably increasing the power of the theory. Archangeli and Suzuki (1997: 206–7) propose to limit such constraints to acquisition, and thus assume that they will 'play no role in the normal input-to-output evaluation'; we return to acquisition in 2.7 below.

(2.10.) $\{V \approx [+\text{high}]\}_I$ Input vowels are $[+\text{high}]$
                                    (Archangeli and Suzuki 1997: 206–7)

Finally, to handle harmony and raising alternations, Archangeli and Suzuki propose Input–Else constraints, which take effect when the input and output structures diverge, allowing input to take precedence over output in evaluation. For instance, in Yokuts, 'Each token of [round] must be linked to vowels of the same height in the input or, lacking an input, in the output' (1997: 215).

Archangeli and Suzuki (1997: 223) contend that 'The ability to characterize such complex patterns of opacity is critical to the success of OT as a theory; it is therefore important that extensions to the model be minimal.' One might suggest that, if the theory were as restrictive and cohesive as it originally made a virtue of being, any addition would be a false step; but this would be a utopian response. More importantly, if these additions are minimal, they nonetheless add a tremendous amount of power to the theory. This power is difficult to assess for two, now familiar, reasons. First, it is unclear whether these constraints are intended to be language-specific or universal, or indeed whether one strategy available to particular languages is to designate a universal constraint as input only or input–else. It is difficult to see how, for instance, Yokuts lowering can be universal, given that it directly contradicts the tenets of faithfulness, and this may be the case for all disparate correspondence constraints, which will then be a further OT analogue of language-specific derivational rules. Secondly, the interaction of these novel constraint types with Gen remains to be determined. Most notably, if we maintain a parallel conception of Gen, which will then provide all possible output candidates, and if disparate correspondence constraints can then in principle link any possible input with any possible output, it is hard to see how the resulting theory could claim restrictiveness, let alone parsimony. Such a model will be equivalent to rule-based theory—and perhaps less constrained than models like Lexical Phonology, where the rules are restricted in scope.

This equivalence with serial derivational phonology extends to a further issue: a disparate correspondence constraint, for instance, 'stipulates the opaque pattern, rather than explaining it' (Kager 1999: 381). Indeed, OT performs less well here, in that even the addition of these extra mechanisms cannot cover cases of opacity which depend on the relationship between the output and some intermediate representation, or a related output form, rather than the input.

One possible solution for certain problematic cases involves Output–Output Correspondence: rather than MAX-IO, DEP-IO and IDENT-IO(Feature), which refer explicitly to Input and Output, we therefore find, for example, MAX-BR, DEP-BR and IDENT-BR(F), which require correspondence between a Base form and its Reduplicant. This extension of correspondence from simple reference to input and output is proposed by McCarthy and Prince (1995); the necessary schema is shown in (2.11.).

(2.11.) Correspondence.

> Given two strings S_1 and S_2, correspondence is a relation $\Re$ from the elements of S_1 to those of S_2.

BR-Correspondence of this type will be invoked, for instance, to deal with overapplication of phonological processes where these involve identity between base and reduplicant. In Malay

(Kager 1999: 233), nasal harmony spreads rightwards, and hence post-nasal vowels are nasal, while all others are oral. However, in reduplication, nasalization overapplies, apparently spreading leftwards: the stem [hamə̃] 'germ' therefore gives the reduplicated plural [hã mə̃ hã mə̃] 'germs'. Kager (1999: 234) here invokes the constraint IDENT-IO(nasal) shown in (2.12.); this is outranked by IDENT-BR(nasal), a constraint identical but for the appearance of B and R rather than I and O. Overapplication is therefore analysed as reflecting a desire for base and reduplicant to be featurally identical.

(2.12.) IDENT-IO(nasal)

>Let α be a segment in I, and β be a correspondent of α in O.
>
>If α is [γnasal], then β is [γnasal].

(Kager 1999: 234)

OO-correspondence can be extended beyond reduplication, and for instance is used by Benua (1995) to analyse truncation. In American English, the hypocoristic forms *Lar, Har, Sar*, shortened from *Larry, Harry, Sarah*, are exceptional on the surface in maintaining [ær]; the usual pattern is for [ɑr], as in *car, lark*, with [æ] surfacing only in closed syllables with other final consonants, or where [r] is heterosyllabic—which of course it is, in the full form of the names. The constraints determining the normal distribution will therefore be outranked by one requiring featural identity between <u>B</u>ase and <u>T</u>runcated form (2.13.).

(2.13.) IDENT-BT(back)

>Let α be a segment in the base, and β be a correspondent of α in the truncated form. If α is [γback], then β is [γback].

(Kager 1999: 261)

Paradoxically, this mechanism of OO-correspondence both increases the power of OT, and is empirically inadequate in various ways. Notably, Klein (1997) argues that OO-constraints cannot deal with reduplication when it involves bound roots. In Chamorro, apart from loans and some native exceptions, stress is typically penultimate. Regardless of stress position in the root, stress is also penultimate under nonreduplicative suffixation; as (2.14.) shows, this may involve apparent stress shift.

(2.14.) nána 'mother'   gúmaʔ 'house'

    dáŋkulu 'big'

    naná-hu 'my mother'   gùmaʔ-níha 'their house'

    dàŋkulón-ña 'bigger'

However, in cases of reduplication, which involves suffixation when the root-final syllable is open (2.15.a.), and infixation when it is closed (2.15.b.), there is no shift of primary stress.

(2.15.) a. dánkolo 'big'   dánkolo + lo 'very big'

       buníta 'pretty'   buníta + ta 'very pretty'

    b. ñálang 'hungry'   ñála + la + ng 'very hungry'

      métgot 'strong'   métgo + go + t 'very strong'

In cases where there is no independent root, reduplication is infixing, and main stress is antepenultimate (2.16.).

(2.16.) dǽla + la + y 'slender, skinny, thin, slim'   *dǽlay

    díki + ki + ʔ 'small, little, diminutive'   *dikiʔ

OO-correspondence will work satisfactorily for cases with a free root, since the placement of stress in this independent form can be ascertained and used to determine a match with the reduplicant. However, it clearly cannot be invoked in the bound root cases; this means no unified account can be given of word-based and root-based reduplication in languages like Chamorro, although these clearly share properties, unless we 'formalize the exclusion of reduplication constraints from the scope of output–output correspondence' (Klein 1997: 713–14). One might go further and consider this an argument against OO-correspondence in general. At the very least, this strategy will be unworkable in cases where some intermediate, non-surfacing form is essential to understanding the character of an actual output. Some of these cases involve phonological opacity; the inapplicability of OO-correspondence here has led to the development of Sympathy theory, to be discussed in 2.6 below. Others, including Klein's Chamorro example, have more to do with morphological relationships and paradigm uniformity, to which we now turn in more detail.

2.5   Morphology–phonology interactions

A great deal of work in phonology during the late 1980s and 1990s has been devoted to interactions of phonology and morphology; this trend is most obvious in Lexical Phonology (Kiparsky 1982; Mohanan 1986; Giegerich 1999; McMahon 2000), which divides the phonological derivation into several sequential levels of rule application: on lexical levels, phonological rules interact with morphological operations, while postlexical phonology works with the syntax. Different phonological patterns can therefore be analysed as depending on, for instance, the relative regularity of affixation, or the native versus borrowed origin of a class of affixes. Precisely these types of interaction, now restated in constraint terms, also require analysis within OT.

One major strategy for handling matches between morphological and phonological domains in OT is alignment, and here there is a clear recognition that language-specific constraint modification will be required. In fact, 'ALIGN is not a constraint, it is a schema for creating constraints' (Russell 1997: 119–20); Kager's (1999: 118) version of this schema is given in (2.17.).

(2.17.) Generalized Alignment:

Align (Cat$_1$, Edge$_1$, Cat$_2$, Edge$_2$) = def

$\forall$ Cat$_1$ $\exists$ Cat$_2$ such that Edge$_1$ of Cat$_1$ and Edge$_2$ of Cat$_2$ coincide.

Where Cat$_1$, Cat$_2$ $\in$ ProsCat $\cup$ GramCat

Edge$_1$, Edge$_2$ $\in$ {Right, Left}

GramCat = stem, word, root, affix, etc.

ProsCat = syllable, foot, prosodic word, mora, etc.

Kager (1999: 119) notes that 'these categories can also be filled by *specific morphemes* in the grammars of individual languages', but justifies the resulting weakening of constraint universality on the grounds that the format of alignment constraints will still be universal, and that only ALIGN is involved (although it is not obvious why alignment constraints in particular should be exempted from universality). For instance, Kager (1999: 122) proposes the constraint in (2.18.) for Tagalog.

(2.18.) ALIGN-*um*-L

Align the left edge of -*um*- with the left edge of the Prosodic Word

This constraint tells us that -*um*- belongs as far left as possible, and hence that it will preferentially be a prefix; however, the interaction of ALIGN-*um*-L with the higher ranking NO-CODA means that, in cases where syllabification of the *m* of -*um*- in a coda would result, -*um*- may surface minimally further right, and appear as an infix. Hence, /um + alis/ gives *um-alis* 'leave', while /um + gradwet/ surfaces as *gr-um-adwet* 'graduate'. Similarly, Rose (1997: 250) invokes the constraint in (2.19.) in her account of second person feminine singular subject marking in Muher and Chaha: note here the further extension of ALIGN to allow reference to a phonological feature rather than a prosodic category.

(2.19.) ALIGN 2SF ROOT R; [front] R

Align the right edge of every 2nd person singular feminine root with the right edge of the feature [front].

A slightly more complex use of ALIGN is found in Merchant's (1996) analysis of German fricative assimilation. Merchant focuses on the distribution of [ç] and [x] in data like those in (2.20.).

(2.20.) Tau-chen   [taʊçən]   'little rope'

tauch-en   [taʊxən]   'dive-INF'

Eunuch [ɔɪnuːx] 'eunuch' ~ Eunuch-ismus [ɔɪnuːçɪsmus] 'eunuchism'

Merchant assumes that the constraint *Aç]$_\sigma$, which disallows coda [ç] after back vowels (and incidentally is another rather language-specific formulation), outranks *[x], which more generally disprefers [x], and that both outrank IDENT-IO[back], which would otherwise require the same value for backness to be preserved in input and output. For intervocalic /ç/ to surface as [x], as in *tauchen*, it must therefore be syllabified in the coda, while /ç/ in *Tauchen* is in the onset; Merchant here invokes ALIGN (Stem, R, σ, R), which aligns the right edge of each Stem with the right edge of some syllable. In *Tauchen*, the stem is *Tau*, and syllabification of /ç/ into the coda would therefore violate the alignment constraint; onset /ç/ here surfaces appropriately as [ç]. In *tauchen*, the stem is *tauch-*, and ALIGN will therefore be satisfied so long as the fricative is in the coda, where it will surface as [x]. In fact, Merchant argues that the fricative in *tauchen, rauchen* is ambisyllabic, and must therefore ensure that ambisyllabic consonants do not violate ALIGN (Stem, R, σ, R); to this end, he introduces a new, additional series of constraints requiring crisp edges.

CRISP (σ), ' ... which requires that all segments be uniquely syllabified' (Merchant 1996: 715), is therefore a less permissive version of ALIGN (Stem, R, σ, R), and their relative ranking in a given language will determine how ambisyllabic consonants pattern. In German, ALIGN (Stem, R, σ, R) ranks higher, so that the ambisyllabic fricative in *tauchen* surfaces as [x]. Finally, in the apparently problematic form *Eunuchismus*, surface [ç] results because ALIGN (Stem, R, σ, R) is specifically formulated to refer to stems; hence, -*chen* and -*en*, which are stem-attaching suffixes, fall under its scope, whereas -*ismus*, which attaches to roots, does not. Since there is no stem boundary, ALIGN (Stem, R, σ, R) is irrelevant to *Eunuchismus*; /ç/ will be syllabified into the onset in response to the ONSET constraint, and therefore surfaces as [ç].

Although Merchant's alignment constraint does not contain reference to language-specific material, it nonetheless encodes a difference in behaviour between two classes of suffixes, which would in Lexical Phonology involve a level distinction. However, there are two difficulties here, one following from the other. First, Merchant's assumption that [x] in *tauchen* is ambisyllabic, whereas [ç] in *Tauchen* is in the onset only, is not based on independent phonetic evidence: the difference between the two forms is arguably morphological, and Merchant is using ambisyllabicity as a diacritic. This raises the more significant problem of how, in OT, morphological differences are to be encoded directly. Merchant's ALIGN constraint refers to stems; but how are we to tell whether a particular suffix attaches to stems or roots, or whether some form is a stem or a root in any case? As Russell (1997: 129) observes, 'It is often tacitly assumed that there is a morphology-like component which chooses the right underlying representations and ships them off to GEN in the phonological component, complete with handy morphological annotations like "Prefix" or "Stem", but little effort has been spent on figuring out what this component is or how it works.'

So long as this is true, there will be even less prospect of providing satisfactory OT accounts of morphology–phonology inter-actions which cannot reasonably be seen as edge effects, and therefore cannot be handled by modifying ALIGN. Pulleyblank (1997: 72) suggests that certain rankings may hold for stems, but others for larger domains including affixes, while Kager (1999: 75) deals with derived environment effects in Indonesian, where certain sequences are permitted root-internally but not across prefix–root boundaries, by assuming that '... faithfulness requirements are enforced more strictly within the root than in non-root morphemes such as affixes.' Along the same lines, Ringen and Vago (1998) propose the positional faithfulness constraint in (2.21.) in their account of Hungarian vowel harmony: this is relativized to apply only to roots.

(2.21.) IDENT-IO$_{harm/root}$

> Correspondent input and output harmonic root vowels have identical specifications for [α back] (harmonic root vowels are those specified as low or round).
>
> (Ringen and Vago 1998: 397)

Kirchner (1996) introduces language-specific material into a well-formedness constraint (2.22.) to deal with a morphologically-conditioned chain shift in Nzebi, contradicting Kager's assumption that only alignment constraints are subject to such modification.

(2.22.) RAISING:

> Maximize vowel height (in verbs when occurring with certain tense and aspect affixes)
>
> (Kirchner 1996: 344)

An alternative, as we saw in the last section, is to invoke OO-correspondence to deal with paradigm uniformity, or surface identity between morphologically related forms which would not be predicted from their phonological contexts alone. In 2.4, we saw that this approach has been proposed for reduplication and truncation; Benua (1995) extends it also to cases of stem-based affixation, notably æ-Tensing in American English. As shown in (2.23.), stems with final [s] have tense [Æ], as do forms with a Class II suffix; but where a Class I suffix is attached, the stem vowel is lax.

(2.23.) pass [pÆs]   ~   passive [pæ.sɪv]

class [klÆs]   ~   classic [klæ.sɪk]

BUT passing [pÆsɪŋ], classy [klÆsi]

Class II affixation only will therefore involve OO-Correspondence between the stem and the affixed form, controlled by the constraint IDENT-BA (tense), which outranks all other constraints in (2.24.); note that Benua refers to the language-specific constraint *æC]$_\sigma$ as a 'descriptive constraint', since it does not generalize to other vowels (Kager 1999: 275).

(2.24.) a. IDENT-BA (tense)

Let α be a segment in the base, and β be a correspondent of α in the affixed form. If α is [γ tense], then β is [γ tense].

b. æ-TENSING
*æC]$_\sigma$ No [æ] in closed syllables.

c. *TENSE-low
Low vowels are lax.

d. IDENT-IO (tense)
Let α be a segment in the input, and β be a correspondent of α in the output. If α is [γ tense], then β is [γ tense].

Of course, this depends again on being able to determine what is a stem, and of the various surface forms involved, which is the base (and therefore has priority in determining the relevant feature value), and which is the derivative. In some cases, as Bermúdez-Otero notes, Benua (1997) has to propose that OO-Correspondence relations are stipulated in the subcategorization frames of affixes, meaning that the base is simply what it is stated to be—no more, no less, and certainly no more generalizable.

OO-Correspondence is also unlikely to help in cases of ranking paradoxes. For instance, take English *keep~ kept*: Prince and Smolensky (1993) attribute the shortening in *kept* to a high-ranking constraint requiring 'good' syllable structure; but this would seem to predict shortening also in *seeped*. Intuitively, faithfulness seems to rank higher for regular verbs than for irregular ones; but this amounts to allowing different rankings on morphological or even lexical grounds. Cases of this sort would be analysed in Lexical Phonology using level ordering, with irregular affixation and the relevant shortening or laxing rule on Level 1, and regular inflection on Level 2. Lin (1997: 421) argues, on the basis of just such ranking paradoxes in Piro, that 'it may be necessary to have constraint evaluations at more than one stage', thus explicitly introducing level-ordering into OT; and Roca (1997: 14) contends that 'multi-level phonology appears inevitable in OT'. This 'interleaved' approach is also integral to Bermúdez-Otero (1999), whose model is primarily a response to opacity, and is presented as an alternative to Sympathy theory, the topic of the next section.

2.6 Sympathy

Recall from 2.4 above that OO-Correspondence, while providing a reasonable descriptive account of those instances of opacity which involve matching two actually surfacing forms, does not generalize to those cases which would, in rule-based theory, have required reference to a non-surfacing, intermediate representation. An example from Tiberian Hebrew (McCarthy 1998*a*: 11) appears in (2.25.).

(2.25.) Underlying Representation: /deš?/

      Epenthesis: deše?

      ? Deletion: deše

Here, the opacity resides in the fact that the context for epenthesis, which operates interconsonantally, is not available on the surface: however, the serial derivation contains the intermediate form *deše ʔ*, where the as yet undeleted /ʔ/ makes the application of epenthesis transparent. In OT, such intermediate representations do not appear, since the 'derivation' is parallel: but as McCarthy (1998*a*: 11) points out, 'a form like *deše ʔ* also has a legitimate status: as a failed member of the candidate set emitted by Gen from the input /deš ʔ/.' What is required, then, is a further extension of Correspondence to allow an output to be faithful to a non-surfacing fellow candidate; in this case, both the output and the failed candidate have the epenthetic vowel in common, as opposed to the input. This extension constitutes Sympathy theory.

Exercising sympathy involves two steps: finding the appropriate failed candidate, and making the output faithful to it in the right way. McCarthy (1998*a*: 11) argues that 'At first glance, selecting the right failed candidate seems like a daunting task, since the set of candidates for any given input is infinite and diverse. But … the relevant candidate is exactly the most harmonic member of the set of candidates that obey a designated input–output (IO) faithfulness constraint.' In the Tiberian Hebrew case, this selector constraint is MAX-C_{IO}, which requires input consonants to be preserved in the output. The candidate which is the object of sympathy, marked in tableaux with a ❀, then exerts its influence over the output via a candidate-to-candidate sympathetic faithfulness constraint, here ❀MAX-$V_{❀}$, which requires all the vowels of the sympathy candidate to appear in the output.

As Kager (1999: 392) observes, sympathy theory adds yet further power to OT, vastly increasing the scope of correspondence, since 'Faithfulness to abstract forms implies a radical increase in the number of constraint interactions, hence in computational complexity of the theory.' This increase might be tempered if sympathy selectors (sometimes marked with ☆) were limited to IO-faithfulness constraints, as McCarthy (1998*a*) suggests; this hypothesis brings the additional advantage of requiring the ❀-candidate to be more faithful to the input than the winning candidate is, so that recoverability of the input from the output might indirectly be improved. However, Bermúdez-Otero (1999), for instance, presents persuasive evidence that in the case of West Germanic Gemination, the sympathy selector would have to be the markedness constraint *[σCj; the number of potential sympathy candidates is then vastly increased, and the claimed advantage for lexical access is lost. McCarthy (1998*b*) attempts a further restriction, replacing the potentially limitless class of inter-candidate faithfulness constraints (the ⊛-constraints of McCarthy (1998*a*)), which specified precisely how the output and sympathy candidates must match, with a single constraint ⊛SYM, 'based on evaluating whether two candidates were produced by the same unfaithful mappings' (1998*b*: 19). This change, however, may add a layer of complexity, since the sympathy candidate and selector constraint are still necessary, and the faithfulness constraints which would have acted as sympathy constraints are presumably still available innately, albeit no longer susceptible to marking as ⊛. However, ⊛SYM is now also independently required, and its status is unclear: although it is stated as a constraint, it seems to operate more like an algorithm, so that its ranking and violability come into question.

Some additional complexity might be balanced, of course, by the loss of other mechanisms previously used in OT to deal with cases of opacity; however, although McCarthy (1998*a*) claims that sympathy provides a unified means of analysing the entire class of opaque phenomena, it does not extend to chain shifts (see Chapter 3 below). Furthermore, even if OO-Correspondence, for instance, were excluded from OT analyses of opacity, it is highly likely still to be employed in cases of morphology–phonology interaction, such as reduplication, where sympathy will not be appropriate. In many cases, there will also be a choice of possible OT analyses, and there is no clear way of determining which of the available strategies should be used: 'in practice, the deployment of anti-opacity strategies in strongly parallel OT is entirely opportunistic and unprincipled' (Bermúdez-Otero 1999: 135). Although sympathy might improve restrictiveness with respect to single analyses, it will therefore not counter the proliferation of machinery in the theory as a whole. This explosion of mechanisms is reflected in the notation, with tableaux becoming more complex and creatively presented by the day: we now find (see Bermúdez-Otero 1999: 14, 146) not only the familiar pointy hands, but pointy hands pointing backwards ☜ for transparent losing candidates, sad faces ☹ for counterfactually losing candidates, stars ☆ and flowers ❀ in cases of sympathy, and unexploded bombs ☒ for counterfactually winning candidates. It is comforting to know that the Wingdings font still includes any number of unused fancy arrows and other arcana like signs of the zodiac, ripe for OT exploitation.

Sympathy also brings potential problems in terms of selecting the selector constraint and the sympathy candidate. McCarthy tells us that the sympathy candidate follows from the selector, since it will be the maximally harmonic candidate satisfying that constraint; but he provides little guidance on how the selector is identified. As Kager (1999: 391) points out, 'the bottom line is that any positive evidence regarding the choice of the selector can only reside in the *opaque form itself*. The learner must infer the choice of the selector from the opaque form. This may seem an unsatisfactory conclusion which has a whiff of circularity.' Similarly, there is a possibility that sympathy necessarily weakens the parallelism of OT, since the output will depend on the sympathy candidate, which might therefore require earlier selection. McCarthy (1998*a*: 20) argues that this does not necessitate serialism, since 'Dependencies of one form on another can also be understood in terms of satisfaction of constraints in parallel … '; but this simply increases our dependence on identifying the selector, especially in view of McCarthy's assumption of a principle of Invisibility (1998*a*: 19), which states that the ❀-candidate cannot be selected with reference to the sympathetic faithfulness constraints, as this risks setting up an infinite loop of mutual dependency.

Even if these difficulties are resolved, there remains the architectural problem that an intermediate representation in rule-based phonology has inherent priority over the surface form, whereas this is not so for a sympathy candidate, which requires stipulation. In general, regardless of the mechanism invoked, OT seems to be treating the symptoms of opacity but failing to identify the

ultimate causes: hence, ' ... at a deep conceptual level, strongly parallel OT cannot make sense of the existence of opacity' (Bermúdez-
Otero 1999: 19). The obvious alternative is to introduce at least a
modicum of serialism into OT, in the form of level-ordering. This
will allow reference to precisely the intermediate representations
required for cases of opacity, and the assumption that constraint
rankings can differ between levels will also facilitate analysis of the
morphology–phonology interactions considered in 2.5 above,
some of which involve ranking paradoxes. Bermúdez-Otero (1999)
proposes Stem, Word and Phrase levels, with constraint hierarchies
potentially differently ranked on each level, but parallel evaluation
within levels: this means that only a very limited number of intermediate representations will be available, namely the outputs of
the first two levels. There are, of course, questions to be answered
before this cophonology approach can be definitively adopted:
most notably, McCarthy (1998*a*: 9) argues that it is 'fundamentally
misconceived' since one might predict that ranking could vary substantially more between levels than actually seems to be the case.
Bermúdez-Otero contends that ranking can be left free, with no
stipulation from UG imposing any limit to discrepancies between
levels, since these will follow from contingent historical events
including, crucially, misacquisition. Surface changes will lead to
reanalyses by language learners, and acquisition, in an interleaved
model, can be sequential, with new rankings at the postlexical level
spreading gradually through the higher reaches of the grammar.
This assumption allows misacquisition to be included in OT, presents opacity as essentially grounded, and models the life-cycle of
variation and change in a way familiar from Lexical Phonology.
Allowing the incursion of contingency, at least in cases of phonological change, will be a major theme of the next chapter.

It is nonetheless true that proponents of level-ordered OT, like
Bermúdez-Otero, will have to assess how the limitations on ranking differences they propose can be maintained if, for instance,
phonological rules as well as constraints are included in OT. More
generally, if we do not accept an interleaved model, and therefore have to contend with the explosion of formal machinery,

constraint types and constraint interactions outlined in this chapter so far, there are very considerable implications for acquisition, to which we now turn.

2.7   Optimality and acquisition

One might initially imagine acquisition to be less of a concern for OT than for most theories of phonology, since the more we assume to be innate, the less needs to be learned. However, even if we accept the strongest possible version of universalism within OT, with absolutely all constraints seen as innate, two major tasks still confront the language learner: ranking the constraints, and internalizing a lexicon.

The literature on learning constraint ranking is based on various algorithms which allow the child to converge on the optimal grammar in a large space of possibilities: recall that we are dealing with a constraint set of unknown size and complexity, even if we do not include mechanisms like local conjunction of constraints (see Chapter 3 below) or OO-correspondence. Matters will be even more complex if we allow truly language-specific constraints and perhaps rules, which will presumably not be innate (see Chapter 5), and which will therefore have to be learnable entirely on the basis of input data. Blevins (1997: 248) argues that 'rules can be learned by generalizing over surface alternations', and shows that the two rules which she considers are so productive, and can be discerned from such readily accessible data, that their acquisition should constitute no obstacle. In other words, so long as we assume the limits on rules which would be expected in any reasonably constrained derivational theory, the rule component of OT will, in acquisitional terms, be the least of our worries. However, in a model of OT with such system-specific devices, acquisition will involve the kind of learning theory appropriate to a derivational model, plus an algorithm for ranking; and since the interaction of rules and constraints in an adult OT grammar has not yet been established, it is hardly surprising that their combination does not yet figure in OT learning theory.

Constraint ranking itself is not likely to be a trivial exercise, in that a relatively small number of constraints will generate a massive number of possible grammars: although 5 constraints will give 120 possible rankings, 10 will give 36 million (Sherrard 1997), and by the time we reach a more realistic system of 50 constraints, the possibilities are well in excess of the 10^{12} cells Aldridge (1996) assumes to compose the average human. It is true that not all possibilities will have to be considered, since in some cases constraints will not be crucially ranked with respect to one another, while metaconstraints may eventually determine the relative ordering of classes of constraints. However, as we saw in 2.2, neither the nature of the metaconstraints nor the definition of these classes has yet been satisfactorily determined; and any progress achieved in these terms is furthermore likely to be counteracted by the explosion in constraint numbers and types reported in previous sections.

It is clear that the learner will need some help, and the main algorithm proposed for acquisition of constraint ranking (Tesar and Smolensky 1998) involves constraint demotion. Here, the child knows the optimal candidate because it is the actually encountered output form, and must structure the grammar to make just that form maximally harmonic, and all competitors suboptimal: 'Constraint Demotion solves this challenge by demoting the constraints violated by the winner down in the hierarchy so that they are dominated by the constraints violated by the loser' (Tesar and Smolensky 1998: 238). Relative harmony is computed by assessing the violations incurred by each candidate and scoring out marks common to winner and loser until only informative cases are left. All this assumes the learner has access to the input form and Gen. In addition, there must either be direct access to all candidates, along with their violation marks (which, as Kager (1999: 302) notes, involves negative evidence, unlikely to be accessible outside the occasional instance of explicit correction), or alternatively, the child must assume that everything outside the actual output is suboptimal, hypothesize other candidates, and compute their violations as part of the learning process. In the latter case, the child will have no direct access to candidates in tableaux except the winner; this may create difficulties for sympathy theory. The learner may also begin either with an unranked constraint set (Tesar and Smolensky 1998) or an initial ranking (Pulleyblank and Turkel 1997); Hale and Reiss (1998) adopt an intermediate position whereby faithfulness constraints begin ranked above well-formedness constraints. In either case, demotion will be a cumulative process, since many outputs will be required to provide the requisite information on ranking for a large constraint set.

An additional complication may arise from the possibility that not all novel constraint types are eligible for ranking in the expected way. Most notably, Archangeli and Suzuki (1997) argue that input markedness conditions are vital in determining the initial representations set up during language acquisition: thus, as we saw in 2.4 above, they propose a constraint making input vowels high to force the underliers /i ii/ for surface [e ee], which are derived using a disparate correspondence constraint with equivalent effects to a lowering rule. However, this input constraint 'plays no role in the normal input-to-output evaluation' (Archangeli and Suzuki 1997: 206), being limited instead to Lexicon Optimization, the process whereby language learners select optimal input forms for the output data they encounter (see below). Since constraints are constraints in OT, with no divisions, for instance, between violable and inviolable or truly universal and effectively language-specific types, we might expect that this restriction to acquisition should be achieved simply by ranking; and indeed, Archangeli and Suzuki (1997: 206) 'assume that this type of *input markedness* constraint must be dominated by its output counterpart.' This, however, entails a different ranking of constraints during acquisition from the one later responsible for day-to-day adult language use; the child must then either unlearn or rerank the input constraints when the lexicon is fully determined (which may be pretty late in the day, given the restriction of certain morphophonemic alternations to learned vocabulary). It would be interesting to test the resultant hypothesis that lexical items learned in adulthood have different input representations, and are affected differently by the constraints, from those with the same surface configurations which are acquired early.

The next question is how the child acquires a lexicon, and here we encounter the main stumbling block for acquisition under OT. Since Gen creates infinite sets of candidates per input, choosing the appropriate input for any given output is potentially extremely complex. The main mechanism invoked is Lexicon Optimization (Prince and Smolensky 1993), which calculates the constraint violations incurred by any particular input–output pair; the best pair will have the fewest violations, and will therefore allow the preferred input to be identified from the output. Input and output will therefore be fairly close, as IO-faithfulness constraints will incur violations whenever the two deviate: an input of /sit/ from output [sit] is likely to be optimal, while /fattttrup/, although corresponding to a possible candidate made available by Gen, will not be selectable by lexicon optimization as the appropriate underlier. Faced with an output [CV], learners will select /CV/ as the appropriate underlier, rather than 'fill the lexicon with supererogatory garbage like /CCVVV/' (Prince and Smolensky 1993: 193).

There are two catches here. First, lexicon optimization is hard to implement for alternating forms, where two or more outputs correspond to a single input in classical generative terms. As Archangeli (1997) notes, the prediction is that exceptional forms will be ironed out, and this is not necessarily the case. Irregularities, alternations and misacquisition are all problematic for learning theory under OT. Secondly, and more centrally, we have already seen that successful constraint ranking depends on access to the inputs: we now discover that postulation of inputs, via lexicon optimization, depends on a ranked set of constraints to provide the necessary lists of violations. As Hale and Reiss (1998: 666) put it, 'We might refer to this approach as the *Teufelkreis* or "vicious circle" theory of language acquisition: the child needs a ranking to get URs and needs URs to get a ranking.' Hale and Reiss further believe most solutions to this paradox to be unacceptable,

depending as they do on extra machinery such as OO-correspondence and constraints directly on the input, which will conflict
with Richness of the Base.

It is impossible to evaluate acquisition under OT fully at
present: issues of constraint ranking cannot be resolved in the
current state of indecision about the types of constraints and
interactions permitted, while Archangeli and Langendoen (1997*b*:
200) characterize the nature of the input as one of the major
unresolved issues in the theory. Since the two are apparently inex-
tricably linked in terms of learning theory, we cannot at present
go beyond the questions raised here. As we shall see in the next
chapter, assuming learned rather than innate constraints does not
necessarily resolve matters, since it simply shifts the balance of
what is assumed to be innate: Hayes (1996), for instance, proposes
constraints which are learnable on the basis of language-specific
evidence, but only if speakers are also assumed to have inherent
knowledge of relative phonetic difficulty. Furthermore, certain
constraint types simply may not be available for grammars if
they must be learned from output data alone: this might in particular be true of banning constraints, which disfavour particular
sequences or structures, and are susceptible to the well-known
problems of negative evidence (Marcus 1993).

In the next chapter, we return in particular to issues of universality in OT. Pulleyblank (1997: 101) contends that 'The claim of
universality, that all constraints are universal, is of interest not
because baroque conglomerate constraints are being analyzed as
"universal", but because simplex constraints, often externally
motivated, can be combined in various rankings to produce richly
different sets of grammars.' We have already seen some examples
of the 'baroque conglomerate' type: we shall see below that even
simplex ones can be dubiously universal, and that differential
ranking, although offering an apparently enlightening approach
to modelling language change, is intrinsically unsatisfactory as an
explanatory mechanism.

3

Constraints, Causation, and Change

3.1 History matters

According to Haspelmath (1999: 22), '... a linguist who asks "Why?" must be a historian.' In certain phonological frameworks, notably Lexical Phonology, the trend towards seeing purely synchronic, distributional factors as the key to understanding grammars, which was so prevalent in the early days of generative phonology, is now being supplemented, or even replaced, by a search for the roots of synchronic phenomena in the history of the language involved: in a sense, introspection is being challenged by retrospection. The question is how far Optimality Theory is or should be in line with these developments, and with associated attempts to model and explain sound changes.

The problems linguistic history creates for models of the OT type will become clear from some of the analyses considered below; but broadly speaking, they involve contingency raising its ugly head. It sometimes seems from the OT literature that the main contribution of history is the creation of messy synchronic residue, which stubbornly refuses to fit into universalist models; and the more language-specific a phenomenon is, and the further removed from clear universal motivations, the more troublesome it will be in OT terms. However, change cannot simply be sidelined or avoided: a more restrictive account of change is essential to any theory, phonological or otherwise, for several reasons. First, if there really are meaningful universal principles, then these should define a space delimiting possible developments.

Secondly, knowing the history of a system can explain otherwise opaque aspects of its current state: a series of well-motivated and clearly conditioned changes can nonetheless culminate in a peculiar and intractable synchronic situation. A purely synchronic account of a system is therefore necessarily partial, and any theory concerned with achieving more complete explanations will crucially have to account for changes and the transitions between systems. Finally, and purely pragmatically, it is not always possible to draw a line decisively between synchrony and diachrony, since there are process types, like epenthesis and deletion, metathesis, and chain shifts, all of which will be reviewed below, which operate both as sound changes and in synchronic phonological alternations. We might then expect Optimality Theory to have something to say about delimiting possible sound change; about the role of the constraints in modelling actual changes; and about the relationship between changes and their synchronic congeners. Indeed, Bermúdez-Otero (1999: 17), working within OT, provides a particularly clear statement of this approach: 'In understanding why grammars are the way they are, one must ... never reject their historical dimension.' That is, to use Bermúdez-Otero's own epigraph, 'History matters'.

3.2   The Cutting Edge: between synchrony and diachrony

3.2.1   *Epenthesis and deletion*

3.2.1.1   Prince and Smolensky (1993)

Sound change did not start out high on the agenda for Optimality Theory: Prince and Smolensky (1993), in their initial, core statement of the theory, do not really consider diachronic issues, and although there has been much more work recently on issues of variation and change within OT, the index to Kager (1999) still does not include references to diachrony, change or sound change. We shall therefore follow the example of the theory in approaching sound change somewhat obliquely, via the discussion of synchronic phonological process-types which are also found historically.

Prince and Smolensky (1993), for instance, propose analyses of synchronic epenthesis and deletion, which can equally result in the addition or loss of segments over time. In cases of apparent insertion or deletion, the constraints involved are crucially FILL and PARSE, paraphrased in (3.1.).

(3.1.) FILL: outputs must be based on inputs, i.e. empty nodes are banned. All nodes must be properly filled.

> PARSE: all underlying material must be analysed, or attached to a node. Unparsed material (i.e. unfilled nodes, and underlying lexical material not attached to nodes) is phonetically unrealized.

If these are globally respected, then clearly FILL will ban insertion, and PARSE will ban deletion; however, they may be violated in the normal way because of higher-ranking constraints. A schematic case is outlined in (3.2.), where (3.2.a) defines a language requiring onsets, and (3.2.b) prohibits codas.

(3.2.) a. Obligatory onsets: input = /V/

> (i) *PARSE—null parse: leave unparsed and hence unrealized. V deletion.
> (ii) *FILL—parse as .□V. C epenthesis.

> b. No codas: input = /CVC/

> (i) *PARSE—leave final C unparsed. C deletion.
> (ii) *FILL—parse as .CV.C□. V epenthesis.

(3.2.a.) shows that for an input structure consisting of a single V, syllabification provides two options which cohere with the requirement for an onset. PARSE can be violated by simply not parsing this vowel; the resulting unattached structure cannot be realized phonetically, effectively resulting in vowel deletion. Alternatively, an empty onset slot can be phonetically realized, violating FILL and achieving results equivalent to consonant epenthesis. Turning to (3.2.b.), it is clear that two strategies again exist for syllabifying an input string of /CVC/ without violating the prohibition on codas. This time, violating PARSE gives consonant deletion by leaving the final C unparsed, while violating FILL creates an empty nuclear slot and hence a second syllable; feature fill-in of some sort instantiates a vowel, giving a percept of vowel epenthesis.

The related real-language case of Arabic, where onsets are obligatory, appears in (3.3.). If there is no onset, a glottal stop is supplied, in violation of FILL. We conclude that ONS dominates FILL.

(3.3.) Arabic: /al-qalamu/ 'the-pen' (nom.)

	Candidates	ONS	FILL
☞	.□al.qa.la.mu.		*
	.al.qa.la.mu.	*!	
	.□al.qa□.la.mu.		**!
	.□al.qal.□a.mu.		**!
	.□al.qa□.la□.mu.		**!*
	.□al.qa□.la□.mu□		**!**.

Our second case is from Lardil, where short noun stems are augmented and long ones truncated in the nominative. In augmentation (3.4.), the optimal parse supplies an empty nuclear slot, contrary to FILL, and phonetic material is supplied. Truncation (3.5.) involves a violation of PARSE in response to the higher-ranking FREE-V, which states that 'Word-final vowels must not be parsed (in the nominative)' (Prince and Smolensky 1993: 101). Because of restrictions on the coda in Lardil, when the final vowel in the nominative is unrealized, preceding consonants are frequently also affected, as in the 'termite' example.

Lardil:

	nominative	nonfuture accusative	gloss
(3.4.)			
	yaka	yak-in	'fish'
	ṛelka	ṛelk-in	'head'
(3.5.)			
	mayǎr	mayǎra-n	'rainbow'
	yukǎr	yukǎra-n	'husband'
	ŋawuŋa	ŋawuŋawu-n	'termite'

The Optimality Theory account of insertion and deletion raises various problems, many of which will recur in further discussion of actual sound changes in the following sections. We might expect an avowedly restrictive theory to provide limits on possible changes, and Prince and Smolensky do argue that epenthesis can take place only in an onset where the nucleus is filled, or in a nucleus where the onset is filled, so ruling out (3.6.).

(3.6.) *.(□)◻C.
'No syllable can have Cod as its only filled position.'
(Prince and Smolensky 1993: 95)

However, epentheses of this kind do seem to occur: there is a very well-known case in Romance, where Latin *schola* gives Spanish *escuela* and French *école*. Prince and Smolensky admit this, accepting that 'we must argue, as indeed must all syllable theorists, that other constraints are involved' (1993: 95); but there is no indication of *what* other constraints. A second difficulty involves providing the right phonetic material in epenthetic positions. Prince and Smolensky say overparsed nodes are 'phonetically realized through some process of filling in default featural values' (1993: 88), entailing that the glottal stop is the default, or maximally underspecified, or unmarked Arabic consonant. Similarly, we assume from (3.4.) that the default Lardil vowel is /a/. For French initial vowel epentheses, like *école, étoile,* presumably the same conclusion follows for /e/, although Durand (1990) analyses several French vowels as more underspecified than /e/, including /i/, /a/, /u/ and schwa. In the case of PARSE violation, underlying consonants or vowels may be unrealized, or underlying long vowels shorten because moras are unparsed, but this may have phonetic consequences, for instance on vowel quality, and it is not clear how we are to account for these; again, we find that many of the syllabic and prosodic aspects of the theory follow from the universal constraints proposed, but the segmental phonology seems to require further and more system-specific mechanisms.

3.2.1.2   McCarthy (1993): constraints and rules

Similar difficulties arise for other OT analyses: for instance, we saw in Chapter 2 above that McCarthy (1993) proposes a rule of r-Insertion for Eastern Massachusetts English on the basis that the intruded [r] is not the default consonant in this system. Such language-specific rules, or marginally less seriously for the apparatus of OT, essentially language-specific constraints of the Lardil FREE-V type, are particularly frequently encountered in OT treatments of sound change and analogous synchronic processes.

Blevins (1997) makes some preliminary suggestions on the relationship between sound changes, constraints, and resulting synchronic alternations; these comments are predicated on McCarthy's (1993) analysis of linking and intrusive [r] in modern English, which he ascribes largely to the two constraints in (3.7.).

(3.7.)   CODA-COND   FINAL-C
         *VrX]σ   *V]PrWd

Blevins attempts to relate the FINAL-C constraint, which disallows lax vowels in word-final position, to the development of historical [r]-Deletion, proposing that FINAL-C 'must have already been in evidence when r/Ø alternations occurred, leading them to be reanalysed as instances of 'repair' for FINAL-C violations'

(1997: 247). She suggests a general schema for reanalyses of this kind, given in (3.8.).

(3.8.) Rule inversion as Constraint satisfaction

Stage I: Constraint C in evidence.

Stage II: Sound change results in surface alternations which can be reinterpreted as instances of constraint-C satisfaction.

Stage III: Alternation is instantiated (often inverted) as a phonological rule indexed to Constraint C.

(Blevins 1997: 247)

What, then, does it mean for a constraint to be 'in evidence'? If constraints are universal and innate (and Blevins 1997: 251 sees her proposals as allowing OT to 'maintain a fixed hierarchy of universal phonological constraints'), then presumably FINAL-C was always present at some level in English, perhaps too low-ranked to have any discernible effect, but nonetheless available. It seems likely, then, that Blevins is suggesting a promotion of FINAL-C to a higher position in the constraint hierarchy. If higher-ranked constraints (and let us for the moment not concern ourselves with the question of how highly ranked a constraint must be to qualify) are 'in evidence', this may mean they have visible effects in the phonology. But this raises a chicken and egg problem of whether these effects arise because the constraint has been reranked, or whether the reranking takes place in response to a change at the data level: this is a central problem for the analysis of sound change as constraint reranking which is now standard in OT, and will be discussed at length in section 3.3 below. Blevins gives a phonetic account of r-Deletion, proposing that 'R-loss as a sound change is a reinterpretation of the vowel-like rhotic glide as a nuclear vowel, due to the acoustic and perceptual similarities of weak rhoticization and central/back/round off-glides' (1997: 232); this cannot then constitute a response to the FINAL-C constraint, or provide a reason for reranking it, although the resulting alternations may fulfil its requirements (see (3.8.) above).

It follows that the argumentation for FINAL-C being 'in evidence' at this stage must then lie elsewhere, perhaps in word-final tensing or lengthening of previously lax vowels. Such changes might be interpreted as evidence that FINAL-C had been reranked: whereas violations had earlier been unimportant, the newly active status of the constraint now provoked remedial sound changes. The reranking itself remains unexplained, however. Conversely, if a prior change of word-final lengthening were to motivate the reranking of FINAL-C by providing visible effects for it in English, we cannot use the constraint to explain the sound change, and will have to seek alternative reasons, perhaps of the phonetic type adduced by Blevins for r-Deletion (and see also McMahon, Foulkes and Tollfree 1994). This will mean that some phonological phenomena, here certain sound changes, are in a sense outside the system of optimality, which may be of some concern given that the synchronic reflexes of these processes are seen as being governed by the constraints, whether or not these need to be supplemented by language-specific rules. Such rules are, in fact, proposed by both McCarthy and Blevins, the latter making the further suggestion that rules are indexed to particular constraints rather than free-standing components of the phonological system.

It would appear, then, that FINAL-C and the sound change of r-Deletion begin as completely independent; it is only when the alternations caused by r-loss are reinterpreted as repairing violations of FINAL-C that an inverted rule indexed to that constraint can be proposed. However, McCarthy (1993) also proposes a second constraint, CODA-COND (see (3.7.) above), which might appear to be more closely linked to the original loss of non-prevocalic [r]: indeed, McCarthy (1993: 172) states that 'CODA-COND is responsible for the loss of etymologic *r* preconsonantally and utterance-finally.' CODA-COND, which outranks FINAL-C, permits [r] only in onsets; and as Blevins (1997: 231) shows, it 'can be motivated both phonetically and typologically'. However, its relation to historical r-loss is again unclear. Certainly, CODA-COND can describe the synchronic situation resulting from the change; but again, we face a difficulty in attempting to deal with the earlier historical situation before r-loss, let alone the transition between the two stages. Since [r] was permitted in codas at an earlier stage, CODA-COND must have been so low-ranked as to be effectively invisible in English. Perhaps, at that earlier period, FINAL-C outranked CODA-COND; forms like *fir, fur, her* would then have final [r] realized even when non-prevocalic, preventing final lax vowels at the cost of a CODA-COND violation (although note that this does not tell us why other forms with lax final vowels were permissible at this stage, and only came to conform to FINAL-C by later tensing). Again, we are faced with the problem of what caused the subsequent reranking. If the two constraints reversed their ranking first, then r-loss could be a response to the newly active status of CODA-COND, but there is no easy explanation for the reranking. On the other hand, if r-loss took place for phonetic reasons, and children learning the language ascribed the synchronic results to the previously dormant CODA-COND, then the relation between the change and the constraint is fortuitous. It is then unclear how much light OT will be able to cast on issues of sound change. Instead, sound change will determine the order of the constraints, and perhaps their form, too, depending on whether we allow changes to introduce new constraints or substantially reformulate old ones in a language-specific way; recall Blevins's (1997) 'unique constraint' requiring trimoraic phrases in Gilbertese, and FREE-V in Lardil. In turn, sound change will require explanation with reference to factors outside OT: we return to these issues in 3.3 below. If certain types of phonological processes, like epenthesis and deletion, are attested both synchronically and diachronically, we must then ask whether explanations internal to OT will suffice at the synchronic level if they fail for equivalent sound changes.

A further complication arises in OT accounts of sound change if we invoke language-specific rules, as we must then understand how such rules come into existence, how they interact with the constraints, and how, if at all, they are affected by reranking: this will be of particular relevance if rules are indeed indexed to specific constraints. Rules at present, and therefore phonological phenomena which require rules, are regarded as somewhat marginal in OT: Blevins (1997: 228) contends that rules 'exist at the periphery' of the grammar, while for McCarthy (1993: 190), a rule is 'a phonologically arbitrary stipulation ... outside the system of Optimality.' Both put English r-Insertion into this class, although in fact this process is supremely natural in the light of its history (McMahon 2000): it is an inverted form of an earlier deletion change. Insertion operates prevocalically because deletion applied before consonants and pauses; hence, precisely non-prevocalically. And it applies after the vowels /ɑː ɔː ə/ because, as a result of earlier sound changes, those were the only vowels after which /r/ could appear at the time of its deletion. Blevins (1997) does observe that the processes she ascribes to language-specific phonological rules, English r-sandhi and Gilbertese nasal sandhi, both involve historical inversion; and McCarthy accounts for the insertion of [r], rather than, say, [t], by invoking reanalysis of [r]-deletion. Rule inversion (Vennemann 1972) has been recognized within Lexical Phonology (Harris 1989; McMahon 1991, 2000) as an important mechanism in the phonologization of low-level sound changes as synchronic phonological rules; but even if practitioners of OT accept the term and the process (which may be unlikely, since McCarthy (1991: 11) contends that rule inversion 'does not characterize any real mechanism of historical change'), it is difficult to define or understand it in a model which has no level-ordering, no distinction between lexical and postlexical phonology, no effective interaction between morphology and phonology, and which gives phonological rules no real status. The fact that the processes requiring rules in OT involve what might informally be called rule inversion is then coincidental and provides no further insight.

But even in cases where a relationship between a historical predecessor and a synchronic rule is recognized, OT analyses encounter problems. Recall that McCarthy's account of linking and intrusive [r] in Eastern Massachusetts English involves the constraints of CODA-COND, and the lower-ranking FINAL-C, as well as a rule of r-Insertion, for which he suggests the two possible formulations in (3.9.).

(3.9.) $\emptyset \rightarrow$ r

     $\emptyset \rightarrow$ r / ---#

These rules are extremely general, and will overgenerate considerably, with extraneous candidates being ruled out by new or existing constraints: this follows from the fact that McCarthy regards phonological rules as language-specific supplements to Gen, which also vastly overgenerates in producing candidates for constraint evaluation. For instance, as Halle and Idsardi (1997: 338) observe, even the more restricted version of McCarthy's rule will derive /sijr/ from /sij/ *see*, and /sijrr/ from /sijr/ *sear.* 'Of course, McCarthy could write a more specific rule of *r*-insertion. But the use of standard generative rules is sufficient to solve the problem, without OT constraints, candidates, and evaluation.' As these initial representations for *see* and *sear* indicate, McCarthy proposes that /r/ remains underlyingly in forms which surface variably with linking [r], but that intrusive [r] represents the application of the rule in (3.9.). For this to work, McCarthy has to make several assumptions: notably, that word-final consonants in English must be ambisyllabic when prevocalic, and crucially, that non-low long or tense vowels are represented with an offglide—hence, /ij uw ej ow/. This means that r-Insertion will automatically be limited to following /ɑ: ɔ: ə/, since these are now 'precisely the non-diphthongal nuclei that can occur word-finally in this dialect of English' (McCarthy 1993: 171). Note that, although Blevins (1997: 230) variously characterizes this set of vowels as lax and short, at least in many varieties the low vowels in *bar, baa, lore, law* are long, and certainly pattern with the long, tense or diphthongal vowels. In some ways, this is unfortunate for

McCarthy's analysis, however, since it is unclear why final long low monophthongs should violate FINAL-C, and why a remedy should be sought in the form of intrusive [r].

Several other problems arise here. First, the interaction between the machinery responsible for insertion and deletion of /r/ on the one hand and schwa on the other is unclear, since although McCarthy (1991), in a partially constraint-based but pre-OT analysis, devoted considerable attention to schwa epenthesis in the context of both /r/ and /l/, McCarthy (1993) does not offer an OT treatment of schwa alternations. Secondly, diphthongal representations for non-low vowels may be appropriate for Eastern Massachusetts, but will be more problematic for other varieties of English, where intrusive [r] occurs in the same contexts, but where some non-low long vowels surface as monophthongs; this is the case for [e: o:] in West Yorkshire, for instance (Broadbent 1991). Additionally, we are no nearer to understanding why only the low long vowels and schwa condition [r]-Insertion, and specifically why the low long vowels lack an offglide. In fact, this seems to be dependent on the history of the system, and explicable only in diachronic terms: earlier changes preceding [r]-loss had left [r] available only after these vowels. This historical happenstance means that attempts to ascribe the constituency of the vowel class which permit intrusive [r] to synchronically accessible phonological factors, for instance by proposing underlying offglides in other long vowels, will neither be explanatory nor even generalizable to other varieties.

McCarthy (1993) argues, on the basis of the distribution of [r] after function words, that [r]-Insertion should not be seen as a hiatus-breaking process, but rather the result of the FINAL-C constraint which applies to prosodic words. His account is therefore opposed to Broadbent (1991), who considers [j w r] as alternative hiatus-breakers introduced by spreading of features from the previous vowel, giving [si:jɪn] *seeing*, [go:wɪn] *going*, [drɒ:rɪn] *drawing*. Although there are difficulties with Broadbent's Government-based account of spreading (see McMahon (2000) for further discussion), the idea that [j w r]-insertion are interacting processes is well supported. For instance, unreduced [o:] will attract a [w] glide, while if it is reduced to schwa, [r] will surface; and further complexities are introduced by [h]-dropping in varieties where this occurs, as shown in (3.10.).

(3.10.) potato and onion

potat[owən] ... or   potat[ərən] ...

Is the potato hot?

potat[ohɒt]   or   potat[owɒt]   or   potat[ərɒt]

Accepting the relationship of r-Insertion with other types of glide formation would also remove the problem that, as Halle and Idsardi (1997: 338) demonstrate, *[sijrɪŋ] is selected as the maximally harmonic candidate on the basis of McCarthy's various constraints: if [j] were seen as a hiatus-breaker and as an alternative to [r] selected according to the preceding vowel, there would be no danger of inserting both (or, in OT terms, of selecting a candidate including both).

Indeed, it may be possible to question the very basis of McCarthy's analysis, namely the assumption that r-final and schwa-final stems must still be distinguished in those non-rhotic varieties of English manifesting both linking and intrusive [r]. Much of McCarthy's evidence here relates to Class I affixes: he assumes that, because [r] surfaces in *Homeric, doctoral, dangerous,* but not in the parallel Level 1 formations *algebraic, aromatic, ideal,* the former must have /r/ at the underlying level, while the latter will not. r-Insertion will then not operate before Level 1 affixes (however that is to be managed in an OT account lacking level-ordering). This division of r-final from vowel-final underliers may not extend to the set with long low vowels: although McCarthy (1993) does not consider this question explicitly, in earlier work he is quite clear that 'No internal evidence of the kind available to language learners would justify an underlying distinction between *spa* and *spar*, which are homophones in all contexts' (1991: 13). We shall therefore concentrate on the forms with schwa.

In fact, on the alternative assumption that *Homer, doctor, danger, algebra, aroma* and *idea* all lack underlying /r/, and that a rule of r-Insertion operates freely on Level 1 and elsewhere, we can still derive the difference between those forms surfacing with [r] and those without. Given that [r]-Insertion applies between a long low vowel or schwa and another vowel, it will operate in *Homeric, doctoral* and *dangerous,* but not in underived *Homer, doctor, danger.* It will not apply in *algebraic* because prevocalic tensing will have produced /e:/ or /eɪ/, which does not constitute an appropriate context for intrusive [r], at the end of the stem. *Ideal* and *aromatic* will also be ineligible for r-Insertion, since in the former case [r] would have to be introduced in the inappropriate context V--C, while in the latter, a [t] appears in the 'r slot'.

McCarthy does not tackle the question of why this extraneous [t] appears, not only in *aromatic,* but also in *operatic, Asiatic* and *dramatic;* nor does he consider why *ideal* should be truncated. If we regard these idiosyncratic suffixes as simply variants of normal Level 1 *-ic, -al,* the conditions on them are hard to formulate: how do we state a restriction that effectively only allows the *-tic* allomorph when intrusive [r] would otherwise surface? There are also various other irregular Level 1 suffixations which appear to block r-Insertion, as shown in (3.11.): the hypothetical [r] forms which 'should' appear are on the left, and the actually occurring derived forms on the right.

(3.11.) *phobia[r]ic   phobic
         *salivara[r]y   salivary
         *opera[r]ic, *drama[r]ic operatic, dramatic
         *stigma[r]ize   stigmatize
         *idea[r]al   ideal

While the *doctoral, dangerous* forms are regularly derived and relatively productive, the forms in (3.11.) show variable clipping or extraneous consonants, and are unproductive and isolated. It may well be that these are not synchronically derived, but are instead learned, stored forms; hardly an uncommon fate for Level 1 derivations. If this is so, then the blocking of r-Insertion here ceases to be a synchronic issue, and becomes a diachronic one: the apparent pre-emption of [r] may simply date from a period when intrusive [r] was not yet available as a hiatus-breaker. This hypothesis is supported by datings in the OED, which reveal that the first attestations of the forms in (3.11.) are invariably early, and precede our first evidence for intrusive [r] in the late eighteenth century. For instance, *stigmatize* is attested from 1585; *salivatory* from 1699 and *salivary* from 1709; and *dramatic* from 1589. Although *operatic* is not attested until 1749, the OED is of the opinion that this is formed analogically on the basis of *dramatic*. More recent or more regular and productive forms, like *with-draw*[r]*al, saw*[r]*ing, baa*[r]*ing, Shah*[r]*ist, banana*[r]*y,* which are Level 2, and *saw*[r]*able, draw*[r]*able, Shah*[r]*ify, quota*[r]*ize, quota*[r]*ization,* which may be Level 1 or 2, do indeed appear with intrusive [r], supporting the hypothesis that its absence from the cases in (3.11.) reflects historical blocking by pre-existing, now stored forms. The advantages of an OT analysis of linking and intrusive [r] over a rule-based account more in tune with the historical development of the system(s) in question are therefore much less clear than McCarthy's discussion would suggest, and do not even include theoretical parsimony if the OT version requires a rule as well as constraints. Indeed, as we shall see in the next section, the rapid proliferation of tools within OT constitutes a more general difficulty for the theory in its handling of phonological phenomena like epenthesis and deletion.

3.2.1.3 Correspondence Theory

It is possible that Correspondence Theory might supply some answers to the questions above. In Prince and Smolensky (1993), Optimality Theory was characterized by the two properties of Strict Surface Orientation, which limits Markedness constraints to statements on the desirability or otherwise of certain properties in the output, and allows Faithfulness constraints of the FILL and PARSE type to refer uniquely to the input and the output forms; and Strong Parallelism, enforcing parallel, simultaneous evaluation by all the constraints in a hierarchy. This distances OT considerably from rule-based derivational frameworks, which allow reference to intermediate representations, in violation of Strict Surface Orientation, and in which serial application of frequently extrinsically ordered rules is the norm. Moreover, Prince and Smolensky adopted the Principle of Containment, according to which the input must be included in all output candidates: note that this does not mean all elements of the input need be pronounced, since some may be left unparsed. However, in subsequent reformulations of OT, notably by McCarthy and Prince, containment is abandoned and the older FILL and PARSE constraints are replaced by DEP and MAX (see Kager 1999: 100 and (3.12.)).

(3.12.) DEP-IO: 'output segments must have input correspondents'

MAX-IO: 'input segments must have output correspondents'

(Kager 1999: 100)

DEP, like FILL, essentially bans epenthesis, while MAX, like PARSE, outlaws deletion (unless these strategies are required, of course, by an over-ruling higher ranked constraint). However, the Correspondence constraints are more malleable than their Faithfulness precursors, since they need no longer simply require an exact match between the input and output, but can be adjusted to specify the type and extent of that match. We consequently also find IDENT-IO constraints which may refer to individual features.

Note also that DEP and MAX in (3.12.) are specified as IO— that is, they refer to correspondence between the input and output forms. The flexibility of Correspondence constraints means that relationships between other pairs of representations can also be incorporated: in McCarthy and Prince's (1995) definition,

'Given two strings S₁ and S₂, correspondence is a relation ℜ from the elements of S₁ to those of S₂.' We therefore find BR-IDENT(F) constraints, requiring identity between base and reduplicant with respect to a particular feature or features, and more generally, OO-correspondence, allowing reference to the characteristics of two output candidates which may be morphologically related, and invoked by Benua (1995) in the treatment of truncation. These cases involve only Faithfulness constraints, but Archangeli and Suzuki (1997) propose a further extension to Correspondence Theory, allowing markedness or well-formedness constraints equally to appear in Correspondence constraints. This presents a new range of possibilities, since different features in input and output may be placed in correspondence: this disparate correspondence is illustrated for Yokuts in (3.13.), and was discussed in 2.4 above.

(3.13.) Lowering: μμIℜO [−high]

> 'Any output correspondent of an input long vowel must be [−high]'

> (Archangeli and Suzuki 1997: 203)

Here, input length corresponds to output non-highness. Kager (1999: 378) refers to this type of disparate correspondence as 'two-level well-formedness', and presents a slightly different case from Tunica, where the correspondence relation involves agreement for certain features between different segments in the input and output strings (3.14.), this time to allow an analysis of vowel harmony.

(3.14.) 'HARMONY-IO

> *If* input V₁ ..... V₂ *then* V₁ and V₂ agree in backness and
> rounding. |
>
> output   V₂

> (Kager 1999: 378)

The relevance of these revised Correspondence constraints to sound changes and analogous synchronic processes is brought out clearly by Kager (1999: 248), who argues that:

... correspondence is not a relationship that is 'established' by constraints, but rather one that is *evaluated* by constraints. Constraints evaluating the *Gen*-supplied correspondence relations are crucially violable, giving rise to optimal candidates displaying imperfect correspondence relations. These imperfections appear as 'deletion', 'epenthesis', 'feature change', 'metathesis', 'partial reduplication', 'skipping', etc.

MAX, DEP and IDENT cannot, however, deal with all these correspondence relations, and Kager therefore also proposes additional Correspondence constraint types, including I-CONTIG and O-CONTIG, which are violated in cases of skipping and intrusion respectively, and LINEARITY, which he defines as an 'anti-metathesis constraint' (1999: 251).

This type of extended Correspondence is obviously extremely flexible, allowing different features to correspond at the same position in input and output, or conversely, defining the same features as corresponding for different input and output positions. When these strategies are added to Output–Output Correspondence, the resulting extensions represent a crucial weapon in the OT armoury against opacity. Although opacity was discussed at length in Chapter 2, it should at least be mentioned again here, since an accumulation of entirely tractable and phonetically conditioned sound changes may create opaque synchronic processes. This means that OT is challenged twice with respect to opacity. First, mechanisms are required to deal with the synchronic fall-out, and these will include the numerous addenda to Correspondence Theory outlined above, plus Sympathy Theory (McCarthy 1998*a,b*) or alternatively, the possibility of interleaved or level-ordered OT (Bermúdez-Otero 1999). The main problem here is that the inflation of theoretical devices and resulting prolixity of choice means OT currently 'suffers from an acute *embarras de richesses*' (Bermúdez-Otero 1999: 109), with a principled division of labour or decision mechanism being required to allow the theory to remain, or become, adequately constrained. Second, OT will only be truly explanatory for such opaque phenomena if analyses of the contributory sound changes themselves can be proposed, and we turn to this issue in section 3.3.

The discussion of Correspondence Theory above relates primarily to challenges to Strict Surface Orientation, but there are also issues involving Strong Parallelism. Specifically, if candidates manifesting various types of disparate correspondence are to be supplied by Gen, and are then evaluated, we must ascertain whether Gen and Eval themselves operate serially, as advocated by Blevins (1997), or in a parallel manner. Prince and Smolensky (1993) prefer a parallel approach, but do mention a serial version, where they argue 'the theory of rules is narrowly circumscribed, but it is inaccurate to think of it as trivial. There are constraints inherent in the limitation to a single operation; and in the requirement that each individual operation in the sequence improve Harmony' (1993: 79). It is unclear whether these restrictions are intended to apply only to synchronic processes as part of Gen; to any synchronic phonological rules required in addition to the constraints; or also to sound changes. If these restrictions do characterize phonological rules or sound changes, more guidance is required on how we define 'a single operation'. It is also unclear that all rules and changes 'improve Harmony'. For instance, in the Lardil example above, we must invoke a historical loss of final vowels in the nominative; this will force a violation of PARSE (or MAX). To what extent, and in what sense, is this truncated form more harmonic than the earlier one with the final vowel? Presumably, the answer has to be that the novel, shorter form is more harmonic given a new constraint system where FREE-V outranks PARSE. Constraint reranking of this type will be the main focus of section 3.3 below.

3.2.2 Metathesis

While epenthesis and deletion vary in the degree of quirkiness of their operation in the phonologies of particular languages, they are at least frequently seen as regular, conditioned sound changes, which may give rise to regular, conditioned phonological rules— or in OT terms, operations controlled by ranked, violable constraints, with or without some of the added panoply of mechanisms discussed above. However, metathesis has typically been seen as more problematic both synchronically and diachronically, being far less easily analysable as a classical, Neogrammarian, ease-of-articulation type of change or the result of such a change. Blevins and Garrett (1998) attempt to reanalyse various categories of metathesis to show that these processes are not necessarily problematic from the point of view of phonetic naturalness. Although one corollary of this approach might seem to be the greater accessibility of metathesis to an OT account, Blevins and Garrett in fact argue that OT is unable to explain these developments, which they attribute to reinterpretation of phonetically ambiguous surface forms.

Blevins and Garrett (1998) consider synchronic and diachronic cases of CV → VC and VC → CV, and divide these into perceptual metatheses, which are restricted to particular segment types, and compensatory metatheses, which are not so restricted, but which typically reduce the number of syllables in a word, and are often stress-conditioned. They define perceptual metatheses as resulting 'when features extending across a CV or VC domain, or perceived as extending across such a domain, are reinterpreted as originating in non-historical positions' (1998: 6); it follows that such metatheses should be limited to segment types characterized by cues with longer durations. Their approach here is partly based on Ohala's (1981) work on dissimilation, which similarly tackles an apparently irregular type of change, and reveals its regularity and motivation by ascribing it, not directly to speakers, but to hearers' mistaken assumptions that those speakers have made a production error. In the case of dissimilation, hearers would assume that an assimilation has been perpetrated, interpreting two phonetically similar surface sounds as reflecting underlyingly more distinct ones: thus, Pre-Shona *bwa 'dog' becomes Shona [bɣa], with the dissimilatory change of labio-velar to velar after a labial reflecting hearers' erroneous hypothesis that the labial has coloured the following segment in production (Ohala 1981). Similarly, in perceptual metathesis, CV or VC where one segment has a feature with a long-duration cue, will be heard as a case of feature-spread with multiple association, and ultimately reanalysed as VC or CV respectively.

On the other hand, the much rarer compensatory metatheses, according to Blevins and Garrett (1998: 33–4), reflect 'a gradual shift of the peripheral vowel articulation towards the tonic vowel'; in other words, there is compensation for the qualitative and/or quantitative weakening of some vowel at the edge of a stem or word, and this compensation takes the form of coarticulation of the stressed vowel under the influence of the weakening one. In this case, the motivation seems to be partly systemic, in that compensatory metathesis tends to happen in languages with rather small and widely-spaced vowel inventories, without many diphthongs or secondary consonant articulations. It is therefore relatively widespread in Austronesian languages.

In both perceptual and compensatory metatheses, then, Blevins and Garrett (1998: 70) hold that 'contrary to the usual view, CV metathesis is just as natural phonetically as other phonological processes. Its segment-transposing effects are phonologically abrupt, but it originates in a very familiar way: an automatic phonetic effect is reinterpreted as phonologically intended or significant.' Metathesis might then seem a good candidate for analysis in a constraint-based framework like OT: but in fact, this conclusion would be rather a hasty one.

First, Blevins and Garrett (1998: 15) contend that 'universal markedness constraints alone cannot easily account for cross-linguistic patterns of perceptual CV metathesis', for three reasons: these metatheses are frequently symmetrical, so that if CV > VC, then also VC > CV, for the same class of consonants; the developments show perceptual phonetic conditioning, and are therefore not explicable purely in phonotactic terms; and considering only the phonotactic dimension does not appropriately delimit the segments and features involved, since it is also necessary to take into account the existence of durationally extended cues. In addition, the actual constraints proposed are often of dubious universality. In his analysis of [TVhR] to [T^{h}VR] metathesis in Cherokee, Flemming (1996) invokes a constraint *h, disfavouring [h]. Blevins and Garrett, however, 'do not see the motivation for context-independent *Seg constraints in general…' (1998: 95 fn.13), and it is easy to sympathize with this point of view on the grounds of relative restrictiveness of the constraint set. That is, if a constraint against [h] exists, why should there not be a similar constraint for every possible consonant or vowel—or indeed, for every conceivable combination? Such negative constraints would arguably not be learnable, and must therefore be innate; this hypothesis is in line with standard thinking within OT, but the challenges involved in acquiring even the ranking of a constraint set of this magnitude would surely be considerable. We shall encounter further *Seg constraints in section 3.3 below. OT analyses of variation, to be considered in 3.4, also often make use of 'exploded' constraints, which may involve factoring out a single constraint like the Obligatory Contour Principle into many sub-constraints, each referring to a single feature. If the constraint shrapnel resulting from such explosions are in fact independent of one another, and can therefore be ranked individually, this will again vastly increase the potential number of constraints to be considered by the child during language acquisition. However, these constraints are at least intended to be universal: some others found in OT treatments of metathesis are much more clearly parochial, as in Hume's (1997: 75) analysis of Leti, where she proposes the constraint '*V: the final vowel of a morpheme in the input may not occur in an open syllable in the output.' Alignment constraints of this sort represent one way of matching up phonological and morphological constituents within Correspondence Theory, and are very commonly characterized by language-specific formulations of this kind: indeed, Kager (1999: 11) argues that the strong assumption of constraint universality has to be 'slightly relativized' for precisely these alignment cases: 'such interface constraints define schemata in which individual languages may substitute their specific morphemes' (1999: 12).

Whether these constraints are innate or not, an issue we return to below, it might be possible to identify their perceptual motivation better by allowing some incursion of the functional and phonetic into OT. Flemming's (1996) *h, for instance, is based on the auditory weakness of [h]—that is, it is a phonetically grounded constraint. However, Blevins and Garrett (1998: 24) again object that it is not enough to identify universal phonetic factors of this kind and restate them as constraints, since 'language learners hearing [TVhR] must have some reason for reinterpreting this as [TʰVR]—some reason which is not a consequence of the phonological constraint system itself, since this is precisely what learners are aiming to acquire.' In any case, a universalist account of this sort may work for one particular language, but it will not always generalize to others with ostensibly similar metatheses: hence, in Zoque, metathesis involves a shift of an intervocalic glottal stop to final position, although glottal stops are certainly more salient intervocalically. There are clearly contingent, language-specific aspects of the changes which are overlooked or concealed in the OT analyses. This will be true of compensatory metatheses too, although in such cases the language-specific conditioning factors are systemic, relating for instance to the number of vowels present and the margin of safety required between them.

These issues go to the heart of the current controversy over phonetic grounding of OT constraints. Hayes (1996: 4) proposes a model of 'Phonetically-Driven Optimality-theoretic Phonology' which differs from the Prince and Smolensky (1993) standard version of OT in that constraints are not inherited, but invented during language acquisition. By a process of inductive grounding, a large number of constraints are hypothesized by the language learner, on the basis of 'a phonetic map of the space of articulatory difficulty' (Hayes 1996: 12). Assuming that 'the goal of a constraint is to exclude hard things and include easy things' (1996: 13), the hypothesized constraints can then be assessed for their degree of grounding, and ranked. This ranking itself will effectively rule out many constraints, which will appear too low in the hierarchy to be of any direct relevance.

As we saw in Chapter 2, Hayes's approach is attractive in lightening the load in terms of innateness: constraints have to be learnable on the basis of the child's input data, rather than prespecified. They will consequently be language-specific, albeit limited by knowledge of universal articulatory markedness. However, a large number of assumptions must be built into the model, and inductive grounding emerges as a lengthy and complex procedure, which will be unable to deal with ungrounded constraints (and, of special relevance for present purposes, with aspects of the language which were once grounded, but are no longer clearly so for reasons of diachronic development). Furthermore, Hayes's proposals are of unclear relevance for changes and processes like metathesis, whose conditioning and motivation is typically perceptual rather than articulatory, since he accepts that inductive grounding is potentially much more complex for perceptually grounded constraints. Whereas articulatory difficulty can be assessed for individual segments, perceptibility will depend on other components of the system, and pairs of entries on the phonetic map will therefore have to be evaluated together, rather than single points. Hayes (1996: 14) therefore does not deal with perceptual grounding, so that his model must be left for future assessment in terms of perceptually conditioned processes: however, given the extra complexity these cases will inevitably involve for his model, and the doubts such complexity already raises for the more straightforward articulatory constraints, it is not clear that inductive grounding will provide a solution.

While Hayes (1996) sees diachronic developments and their residues as a source of exceptionality for inductive grounding, Haspelmath (1999) considers these issues as central to the formulation and motivation of constraints. Essentially, Haspelmath argues that grammatical optimality must be supplemented by user optimality in order for us to understand why certain constraints are proposed rather than their inverses—why we find NOCODA and ONSET very frequently in the literature, for instance, but not CODA and NOONSET. Certainly, OT is attractive in that 'many of the constraints are intuitively plausible, and because the description in terms of the "best" and "worst" candidates often corresponds to our pretheoretical feelings' (Haspelmath 1999: 2); but formalizing those intuitions in constraint terms is only really explanatory or revelatory if we also understand what lies behind both the constraints and the intuitions.

Haspelmath (1999: 5) grounds OT constraints in terms of user optimality, arguing that 'the best option among a range of alternatives is the one which promises the highest net benefit to speaker and hearer.' He assumes that variants arising in historical change are subject to functional selection, with speakers and hearers able to judge which form suits them best, and that form ultimately coming to dominate as the new standard variant. OT constraints used to describe that resultant synchronic situation therefore have the shape they do as a result of what Haspelmath calls 'diachronic adaptation'. To take one example, NO VOICE CODA, which in a standard OT definition would state 'Voiced coda obstruents are forbidden', is related to 'User-optimal NO VOICE CODA: Coda obstruents should be pronounced voiceless in order to avoid articulatory difficulties' (Haspelmath 1999: 13). Hence, the synchronic constraints relevant to a particular system will depend on the interaction of the history of that system with the language user's knowledge of what is 'better' or 'worse' for speakers and hearers; and Haspelmath argues that the constraints themselves are not innate. In this sense, Haspelmath's diachronic adaptation scenario overlaps with Hayes's (1996) inductive grounding.

Haspelmath's proposals raise various issues. First, although he is quite clear that OT constraints need not be innate given diachronic adaptation, Haspelmath tells us less about the status of the phonetic knowledge on which user optimality depends. Being universal, it might be expected to be innate, and therefore a product of the biological evolution of language (see Chapters 4 and 5 below); again, this would bring Haspelmath's views close to Hayes's. However, Hayes raises relevant questions here, noting that some constraints are phonetically grounded but refer to very rare sounds. For instance, Steriade (1995) has proposed that retroflexes and preglottalized sonorants are preferentially post-vocalic for phonetic reasons, but in Maddieson (1984), 66/317 languages surveyed had retroflexes, while only 20/317 had any laryngealized sonorants; and 'There is no selective advantage to possessing an innate constraint on the distribution of retroflexes if the language you are learning doesn't have any' (Hayes 1996: 26). Hayes proposes therefore that the constraints are input-based, so that a constraint on the distribution of retroflexes will be hypothesized by learners just in case there are some, and their distribution is restricted. In Haspelmath's work, however, the difference is not entirely clear between hypothesizing an innate constraint with a particular effect on the one hand, and proposing that such a constraint could be formulated if required, but crucially on the basis of innate, universal phonetic knowledge telling language users what would be wrong for example with prevocalic retroflexes if there were any.

Haspelmath also notes that certain OT constraints will not be good candidates for reformulation in terms of user optimality: these will include language-specific constraints, and any constraint pairs with the two parts working in opposite directions. He notes that ' ... these constraints clearly have the flavour of theoretical constructs that help make the particular analysis work, but that would be the first candidates for elimination if this becomes possible' (1999: 5–6). It does not seem likely, however, that this will work as a filter for unsuitable constraints: ruling out any proposed constraint on the grounds that it does not have a functional, phonetic basis either means sidelining the fact that certain synchronic phonological processes will not be transparently conditioned in this way, or finding a second mechanism to describe such processes—rules as opposed to constraints, for instance. Furthermore, it seems Haspelmath is asking us to consider OT not on its current merits, but by ignoring problematic elements of the theory which are in common use, but which he recognizes as undesirable. It is surely essential to carry out a reasoned evaluation based on the way the theory actually is, rather than giving its practitioners credit for realizing that certain mechanisms are undesirable, while they nonetheless continue to use them.

Finally, Haspelmath's contention that diachronic adaptation is relevant to the formulation of OT constraints arguably goes through only on the assumption that OT can actually model sound change. If we are to see variation and change as crucially accounting for why constraints have the shape they do, then to be a complete theory of phonology, OT must demonstrate that it can analyse these appropriately, especially given the overlap between synchronic and diachronic process types explored above for epenthesis, deletion and metathesis, for instance. This does not always appear to be so, even when we consider only the few cases reviewed above. For instance, if Haspelmath is correct, we might expect McCarthy's analysis of linking and intrusive [r] to involve constraints that reflect its historical sources. However, although there is a clear phonetic rationale for the historical loss of [r], which might be statable in terms of user optimality (see McMahon, Foulkes and Tollfree 1994), this is not reflected in the constraints McCarthy employs to account for the synchronic pattern—and indeed, as we have seen, constraints are insufficient in any case, and McCarthy is forced to supplement these with a rule. Blevins and Garrett (1998) make a similar point on metathesis, which on their analysis has a transparent phonetic history, but which is problematic for OT in synchronic terms, requiring use of just those mechanisms, notably language-specific constraints, which Haspelmath identifies as undesirable. Simply incorporating phonetic motivation into OT, in whatever way, is therefore not necessarily a panacea for processes like metathesis.

Blevins and Garrett (1998: 72) conclude their discussion of metathesis by identifying 'a major conceptual difference' between their own account and possible OT analyses, despite the fact that both make use of the results of experimental phonetic research. In OT, a CVh > ChV metathesis will probably be ascribed to a constraint against Vh, which in turn, in versions including phonetic grounding, will be motivated by the knowledge that [h] is harder to hear postvocalically than prevocalically: 'Perceptual optimization is thus the cause of metathesis: a change happens because the resulting sequence is easier to hear' (Blevins and Garrett 1998: 73). It is easy to relate this approach both to Hayes's idea that 'the goal of a constraint is to exclude hard things and include easy things' (1996: 13), and to Haspelmath's user optimality. However, in Blevins and Garrett's view, the metathesis is caused by misinterpretation, which in its turn is provoked by the long durational cues for [h], and the difficulty of hearing [h] postvocalically: under these circumstances, it is natural for those cues to be reinterpreted as originally prevocalic. Both analyses therefore hinge on lack of perceptibility; but as Blevins and Garrett (1998: 73–4) note:

the optimization account treats perceptual ease as the GOAL of the change, requiring that language learners have some knowledge of the relative perceptual ease of sound patterns (e.g. in the form of Optimality Theory constraints). This need not be assumed in our account. We assume only that what is hard to perceive is sometimes not perceived, and that misperception leads to misinterpretation and change—assumptions which are independently needed (unless language learning is uniquely error-free among human activities).

Seeing the motivation for a change as also constituting its goal runs a serious risk of teleology (Lass 1980): historical linguists tend to avoid characterizing changes as taking place in order to provide a particular outcome, for exactly this reason. In the next section, we shall explore the mechanism of constraint reranking, a response to some change already taking place on the surface. Here, however, we seem to be facing the opposite situation, with a change happening to ensure or increase coherence with a particular constraint or hierarchization, which clearly seems goal-directed. Blevins and Garrett's assumption that error and misinterpretation are at issue necessarily introduces contingency and language-specificity, regardless of the ultimately universal, phonetic motivations involved; we shall see that, paradoxically, this represents a step forward in the context of language change, where general principles alone are insufficient and often unenlightening.

3.2.3   Chain shifts

Chain shifts appear to fall into the same category as metatheses as far as Optimality Theory is concerned: they initially seem promising candidates for a constraint-based analysis, but further and more detailed study reveals serious and recurrent difficulties for OT. Again, we turn to historical chain shifts, and notably the Middle English Great Vowel Shift, in 3.3; here, we shall concentrate on synchronic chain shifts, and cases of change in progress.

Labov, surely the authority on this area, holds that 'When a number of English dialects are charted, and when these results are compared with the array of chain shifts reported in the historical record, constraints emerge with a compelling, exceptionless character that would satisfy the most stringent demands of a universalist approach' (1994: 115–16). Some of the principles Labov formulates on the basis of both historical and ongoing chain shifts are given in (3.15.).

(3.15)   'In chain shifts, peripheral vowels become more open and nonperipheral vowels become less open.'

'In chain shifts, low nonperipheral vowels become peripheral.'

(Labov 1994: 601–2)

Some of Labov's principles are taken to govern chain shifts in general; others are specifically stated as Exit Principles, which govern the behaviour of the leaving element(s) in a system, which are unable to progress further along the trajectory of the shift within the existing system, and which may therefore lengthen, shorten, monophthongize or diphthongize. In cases where these potential exits from a system are closed, mergers will necessarily result, as in Greek, where eight historically contrasting vowels fall together as /i/ (Labov 1994: 271). Nor are the principles illustrated only with English data: for instance, Labov shows that symmetrical raising and diphthongization, though perhaps best known in the context of the Great Vowel Shift, is also manifested in Czech,

Old Prussian and Middle High German, while raising plus fronting is another repeated pattern found, for instance, in chain shifts in Germanic, Albanian, Lithuanian, and the Lolo–Burmese language Akha.

Nonetheless, Labov does provide extensive illustration and justification of the principles in the context of the ongoing Northern Cities Shift in US English. This process, which, as its name suggests, is furthest advanced in big cities like Buffalo, Cleveland and Chicago, is of particular interest because (Labov 1994: 178)

It is the most complex chain shift yet recorded within one subsystem, involving six members of the English vowel system in one continuous and connected pattern. It is also a remarkable new development in English phonology: over the past millennium, most of the rotations have affected the long vowels; the short vowels have remained relatively stable.

The whole pattern of the Northern Cities Shift, in its most complete form, is given in (3.16.), with some examples of its effects. However, although this series of steps shows the consequence of the completed shift for the system, it does not reflect the order in which the steps took place: Labov (1994: 195) argues that raising and fronting of /æ/ appears to have been the first step, followed by subshifts of /o/, /oh/, /e/, /i/ and finally /ʌ/, this last stage being apparent first in recordings from the late 1970s and early 1980s. He analyses all these subshifts as involving fronting of tense vowels along peripheral paths, and backing of lax vowels along nonperipheral paths, a view which, incidentally, allows resolution of certain failures of vowels to merge when this might have appeared inevitable from ongoing changes, since a vowel on a peripheral track may pass another shifting on a nonperipheral track without colliding.

(3.16.) The Northern Cities Shift: i → e → ʌ → oh → o → æh → iy

        Debbie, steady = [dʌbi], [stʌdi]   got = [gæht]

        massive drop = [mɛsɪv drap]

Initially, Labov's observations on chain shifts appear to fit well into an OT approach, an impression strengthened by his contention that none of these principles is exceptionless: processes exhibiting just such general but violable trends might seem naturally characterizable by OT constraints. However, there are various difficulties which make the match between chain shifts and OT less close. First, Labov (1994: 140) argues that social factors very largely determine when the principles of chain shifting are adhered to: OT constraints respond to innate, phonological universals rather than contingent social pressures, a consideration also relevant to Optimality accounts of language variation, as we shall see in 3.4 below. Second, chain shifts are also powerfully systemically and phonetically conditioned: for instance, issues of avoidance of merger and preservation of distinctions are involved, while discrepancies between front and back vowel shifts may arise from the greater available articulatory space for front vowels, meaning that four degrees of height, for instance, are more readily sustainable at front than at back position. These functional and phonetic issues raise the same difficulties for an OT analysis of chain shifts as for compensatory and perceptual metathesis, which, as we saw earlier, are equally conditioned by systemic and phonetic factors respectively.

Finally, 'Synchronic chain shifts, whereby certain sounds are promoted (or demoted) stepwise along some phonetic scale in some context, are one of the classic cases of opaque rule interactions' (Kirchner 1996: 341). Although diachronic chain shifts (and chain shifts in progress, like the Northern Cities Shift) can be dealt with by assuming that the various stages are historically sequential and non-overlapping, cases where synchronic alternations seem describable in terms of chain shifts are much more problematic for OT for reasons of apparent ordering and reciprocity. That is, a chain shift with /a/ → [e] and /e/ → [i] can be handled by sequential rule ordering with /e/ → [i] first, to avoid the otherwise predicted merger; but in a strictly parallel instantiation of OT, this ordering cannot be modelled. Furthermore, if we dealt with /a/ → [e] in a standard OT manner, by invoking constraints favouring [e] rather than [a], it is inexplicable why [e] should then simultaneously be disfavoured in the same context, being replaced by [i].

Various methods of dealing with chain shifts in OT terms have been proposed: Kirchner notes, for instance, that McCarthy analyses the Bedouin Hijazi Arabic shift illustrated in (3.17.) as reflecting a constraint NO-V-PLACE, which prohibits place feature specifications for short vowels in open syllables, thus producing vowel reduction, in association with various PARSE constraints and an assumption that stray elements are automatically deleted postphonologically.

(3.17.) Bedouin Hijazi Arabic:

/a/ → [i], /i/ → Ø in open nonfinal syllables

/kitil/ = [ktil] 'he was killed'

/katab/ = [kitab] 'he wrote'

However, Kirchner argues that this approach cannot be extended to chain shifts with more than two steps, or cases where there is no deletion, as is the case in the Bantu language Nzebi, where /a/ → [ɛ], /ɛ/ → [e], and /e/ → [i]. In this case, Kirchner initially suggests the morphologically conditioned constraint 'RAISING: Maximize vowel height (in verbs when occurring with certain tense and aspect affixes)' (1996: 344), another language-specifically customized constraint of the type frequently associated with opaque alternations and historical changes. This, however, turns out to be unsatisfactory, since 'there appears to be no way to rank RAISING relative to the $PARSE_F$ constraints to permit raising of the nonhigh vowels without raising /a/ all the way to [i]' (Kirchner 1996: 345). Kirchner therefore proposes a new strategy allowing local conjunction of constraints: this allows multiple violations of a single constraint or related ones to be assessed, since a derived constraint will be violated only if all its component, conjoined constraints are violated. Hence, $PARSE_{low}$ and $PARSE_{ATR}$, and $PARSE_{high}$ and $PARSE_{ATR}$ could be locally conjoined, allowing the Nzebi chain shift to be modelled.

The objections which might be raised here are perhaps predictable. Again, we face a proliferation of analytical techniques and of constraints within OT. Local conjunction must be added to the various novel subtypes of Correspondence and to Sympathy Theory to deal with opacity, and there seems no principled way of deciding which should be applied in particular cases beyond trial and error. It is not even possible to argue that local conjunction can deal in a unified way with the entire class of chain shifts, since Kirchner (1996: 348, fn.8) himself observes that circular chain shifts do not lend themselves to analysis in this way: this would include the Northern Cities Shift, for instance, and Xiamen tone sandhi (Chen 1987), where contour tones shift in the sequence $53 \rightarrow 44$, $44 \rightarrow 22$, $22 \rightarrow 21$, $21 \rightarrow 53$. Kirchner (1996: 348) accepts that 'Unrestricted local conjunction would appear to result in excessive descriptive power'; it is also certain to increase the number of constraints, since if a violation of a conjoined constraint is more serious than violation of its components, this implies both that the conjoined constraint and the components are individually present in the hierarchy, and that the conjoined constraint outranks the component constraints. This will have two possible consequences. If conjoined constraints are innate, the number of constraints which require ranking will rise considerably, since presumably all possible local conjunctions must be innately available unless some principled division can be drawn between those constraints which are conjoinable and those which are not (and Kirchner recognizes that this is not currently possible: hence, it is not clear whether more than two constraints can be locally conjoined, or if composite constraints can be made up of a combination of faithfulness and markedness constraints, for instance). On the other hand, if local conjunction is language-specific, and children learning a language decide to conjoin innate constraints as a response to particular input data during acquisition, then we must again confront the question of how universal constraints and language-specific modifications interact, and how innate and hypothesized constraints are to be ranked into a single hierarchy. Finally, Kager (1999: 400) identifies a more philosophical problem, in that local conjunction 'seems to stipulate what should come for free in OT, given the architecture of the theory.' That is, the existing system of evaluation ought to filter out the 'worst-of-the-worst' forms with more violations than necessary in any case: this is precisely the kind of situation for which a new mechanism should not need to be formulated within OT.

3.3   Constraint reranking and the explanation of change

3.3.1   *Modelling sound change in OT*

In the next two sections, we turn to the modelling of sound change proper within OT, and to the associated issue of how variation is to be captured in a constraint-based model. This concern is a relatively recent one for formal phonology in general, and not just for OT: as Anttila and Cho (1998: 31) put it,

Variation and change have not been among the leading issues in generative linguistics. While generative grammar is concerned with competence, variation reflects interactions between competence and other cognitive systems, including social systems, whereas change is often manifestly driven by external factors such as language contact. The question arises as to what extent grammars, construed as synchronic, psychological entities, play a role in language variation and change.

Various arguments adduced in earlier sections make the case for considering change and a model of change as a necessary component of a phonological theory; and there has certainly been a recent *de facto* adoption of this attitude within OT, with Hinskens, van Hout and Wetzels (1997), Zubritskaya (1997), Anttila and Cho (1998), Green (1998), Miglio (1998), and Bermúdez-Otero (1999) all representing contributions to the nascent field: all these will be discussed further below.

Turning first to sound change, one main mechanism is invoked in OT to account for grammatical, and therefore surface, phonological change: this is constraint reranking. Archangeli (1997: 31) makes this point quite unambiguously: 'Under OT, the formal characterization of language change through time is that constraints are reranked.' Of course, it makes supremely good sense for OT to model change in terms of constraint reranking, for two reasons. First, cross-linguistic variation is captured in terms of different rank orders, and there seems no good reason why this should not hold diachronically as well as diatopically. Second, if we follow the standard OT assumption that constraints 'are not arbitrary stipulations plucked from the air to produce the correct results; every constraint should articulate a universal linguistic tendency' (Sherrard 1997: 45), then we are not at liberty to propose the addition or deletion of constraints or, taking the strictest possible line, the modification of existing constraints either. If constraints cannot be gained, lost or altered, and if they are the only formal object of phonological analysis within OT, then there are very few options for the treatment of sound change beyond reshuffling them. In short, diachronically as well as synchronically, 'The constraints provided by Universal Grammar are simple and general; interlinguistic differences arise from the permutations of constraint-ranking; typology is the study of the range of systems that reranking permits' (Prince and Smolensky 1993: 5).

I shall argue below that in accounting for sound change, universal constraints and constraint ranking alone are not enough. At best, we find that these systems of OT can describe what happens in sound change. It is true that this is equally all phonological rules can typically do, but the difference is that rules are not presented, or intended, as directly explanatory: they have a language, and indeed dialect-specific role in describing processes, which require explanation externally, perhaps in terms of history, phonetics, memory or acquisition. On the other hand, the Optimality Theoretic account of sound change is not generally presented as a descriptive system: it seems categorically intended as an explanatory one. For instance, the abstract to Miglio (1998) tells us that 'This paper presents a model of the Great Vowel Shift ... and offers an explanation of how it may have been triggered ... The model shows how Optimality Theory ... can be ... an important means to explain language change ... The novelty of the paper consists in explaining what may have set [the change] off ... This is a natural explanation ...'. Sherrard (1997: 82) supports this impression with his assertion that, while rule-based phonology 'typically tells us *what* happens in a language', OT 'arguably places greater emphasis on *why what happens happens* by supplying priorities and objectives for the grammar'.

An obvious difficulty arises if these claims for the explanatory nature of OT turn out not to be fulfilled. Worse than this, however, OT cannot always even describe sound changes or their synchronic aftermath: in particular, we have already seen cases, and will encounter more below, when extra mechanisms—either effectively language-specific constraints, or actually language-specific rules—are required to model the messy residue sound change often leaves behind. I would like to stress too that these problems intensify as we move away from prosodic issues and syllabification, where the contribution of OT is perhaps more secure, and towards segmental and particularly morphophonological processes.

In order to assess whether the OT model of sound change can indeed explain why what happens happens, via constraint reranking and interaction, we turn now to a series of case studies from the literature.

3.3.2   The Great Vowel Shift: Miglio (1998)

In 3.2.3 above, we saw that synchronic chain shifts, and chain shifts in progress, constitute something of a challenge for Optimality Theory. This turns out to be no less the case for completed, historical cases. Miglio (1998) attempts an OT analysis of perhaps the best known of these, the Middle English Great Vowel Shift, with its circular pattern for both front and back long vowels. Circular chain shifts of this sort are particularly problematic for any theory cast in terms of markedness, since they are unconditioned, and furthermore involve swopping of feature values in the same environment, so that considerations of articulatory or perceptual preference are difficult to invoke. That is, what sort of constraint or constraints would make the occurrence of long vowels A to Z in lexical classes A to Z maximally harmonic at time t1, but a different distribution of long vowels A to Z in lexical classes B to A at time t2, with the system of vowels remaining very substantially unchanged?

Miglio's answer is that weak points in a system, defined in terms of markedness and ultimately perceptually, can be identified as probable causes of change. Miglio argues that /ɛː ɔː/ constituted the weak spots in this case: mid long lax vowels of this type emerge from Maddieson (1984) as rare, and therefore highly marked. She proposes that, although these vowels had been part of the English vowel inventory for a long period, 'the shift and instability of these lax long vowels was perhaps primarily caused by the coming into the inventory of a bulk of lexemes with these vowels caused by the Middle English Open Syllable Lengthening'; if children are sensitive to major changes in the functional load of segments, then 'these words with newly lengthened vowels may have caused the demotion of a faithfulness constraint or promotion of a markedness constraint against mid long lax vowels' (1998: 3).

Miglio (1998) requires various Faithfulness constraints of the IDENT$_{[hi]}$ type, plus well-formedness constraints like *MID [-ATR], which disfavours mid lax vowels, and crucially, a co-occurrence constraint *[-ATR]mm, which expresses the markedness of long lax vowels. Although Miglio's account does not make this explicit, it would appear that the influx of words with /ɛː ɔː/ after MEOSL must have caused the reranking of *[-ATR]mm, which had earlier ranked too low to provoke any reaction to the marginal presence of these vowels in the system. The consequent raising of /ɛː ɔː/, however, only starts a chain shift because of a further constraint, DISTANCE, which is itself composed of two constraint families, Maintain Contrast and Mindist, the latter 'requiring a minimal auditory distance between contrasting forms' (Miglio 1998: 9). This constraint, which favours the avoidance of mergers, must be ranked fairly high in Middle English to encourage the continuation of the Great Vowel Shift; where it is ranked low, vowel mergers would be predicted instead.

However, this combination of constraints still does not allow Miglio to model part of the Vowel Shift, namely the raising of /aː/ to /ɛː/. To account for this, Miglio has to assume that the top part of the Great Vowel Shift took place, then a change in the grammar caused the demotion of *[-ATR]mm, along with the promotion or introduction of a local conjunction of faithfulness constraints referring to height and [ATR]: this 'allows /aː/ to raise, but not as far as [eː]' (1998: 11). Since precisely such a raising to [eː] does happen subsequently during the Vowel Shift, there must presumably be yet a further reranking of some sort at a later stage, reactivating the dispreference for /ɛː/ which, in Miglio's view, motivated the initial shift in the first place.

There are various difficulties with Miglio's account, even leaving aside the now-familiar concerns over the proliferation of theoretical apparatus (with local conjunction of constraints, and functionally motivated constraint families both making an appearance here). First, Middle English Open Syllable Lengthening does indeed represent a source of additional vocabulary with /ɛː/ and /ɔː/, but the extra frequency of these highly marked vowels seems to have gone unremarked for some time: that is, MEOSL is generally accepted as preceding the Great Vowel Shift by around 300 years, or several generations of speakers, during which time /ɛː ɔː/ were stable members of the system. Why should such a period elapse before the onset of raising? A second difficulty also involves the initiation of the change, and the mechanism of reranking. Miglio treats /ɛː/ and /ɔː/ together in her discussion of the initial raising which begins the Vowel Shift, and the various constraint rerankings she posits necessarily affect them both. However, at the end of the Great Vowel Shift, although /ɛː/ had been removed from the system, /ɔː/ remained. Presumably yet another reranking would have to be posited, demoting the constraint disfavouring long lax vowels after /ɛː/ had raised but before /ɔː/ had; or some differentiation between back and front vowels would need to be built in, resulting in more, or more complex, constraints.

With this in mind, it is important to ask what the motivation is for the particular constraints Miglio selects in her analysis of the

Great Vowel Shift. In Miglio's defence, she does not propose individual constraints which seem language-specific, although her use of local conjunction raises again the question of whether all possible conjunctions are available 'prepacked', innately, or whether only the subconstraints need be posited as innate, while their combinations can be learned in response to language-specific data. Her constraints are clearly intended to be motivated, either functionally and phonetically, as in the case of Distance and its subparts, Maintain Contrast and Mindist, or typologically, as with *[-ATR]mm and *MID[-ATR], which she explicitly grounds on frequency counts from Maddieson (1984). However, one might equally analyse the Great Vowel Shift in terms of other constraints with the same type of motivation, such as those in (3.18.).

(3.18.) a. $V \approx [+high]$: vowels are high.
        b. NO-MERGER: keep contrastive vowels maximally distinct.

(3.18.a.) would account for a drive towards vowel raising, which might be tempered by (3.18.b.), preventing a wholesale collapse. The Great Vowel Shift could then be attributed to a reranking of $V \approx [+high]$ relative to the earlier dominant NO-MERGER, which had previously kept each vowel in its place. NO-MERGER, like Miglio's Distance, is functionally and systemically motivated; $V \approx [+high]$, on the other hand, like Miglio's *[-ATR]mm, is typologically based, and reflects the common emphasis in the OT literature on cross-linguistic attestation of phonological phenomena which can be attributed to a particular constraint. In this case, precisely constraint (3.18.a.) is proposed for Yokuts by Archangeli and Suzuki (1997: 200). Since both analyses involve similarly motivated constraints, and both, in standard OT fashion, require reranking, we must confront the question of what sort of pathway an argument would take within OT for assessing the superiority of one over the other. In rule-based phonology, an account will be judged on whether the rules proposed do or do not capture the facts of the language, with explanations coming necessarily from beyond those rules. In OT, the idea of deriving both description and explanation from the innate constraints is attractive; but there are currently so many candidate constraints which could be used and combined in so many different ways, that it is hard to see how we are to tell when we have found the right analysis. Many analyses therefore reduce to exercises in constraint invention, in the absence of any sensible limit on the form and number of constraints to be proposed.

In addition, explanation for the sound change(s) still appears to be theory-external in many cases. For instance, although Hayes (1996) sees many constraints as necessarily grounded phonetically, they are based on universal phonetic knowledge which is separate from the constraints themselves: Hayes (1996) and Haspelmath (1999) also consider their constraints to be learned rather than innate, meaning that typological data on frequency and so on is no longer so directly relevant in their formulation. One might favour an OT analysis on the grounds of greater economy or parsimony, which seems justifiable in a theory which prides itself on the replacement of rules plus constraints with constraints alone; but again, it is unclear how this is to be assessed. Would an analysis with fewer constraints, but more complex ones (for instance, involving local conjunction) be preferable to one with more, simpler constraints? How does a language-specific constraint count as against a universal one, and does it matter whether the language-specificity is total, or involves modification or parametrization of a more general constraint or schema? Inclusion of variant mechanisms like disparate correspondence, local conjunction, and Sympathy can only muddy the waters further here; and matters become arguably even worse when we turn to the synchronic residue of the Great Vowel Shift, in the form of *divine ~ divinity*, *serene ~ serenity* alternations. Psycholinguistic evidence (Jaeger 1986; Wang and Derwing 1986) suggests that some speakers at least have a Vowel Shift concept, corresponding to a constrained version of the SPE Vowel Shift Rule (McMahon 1990). However, these synchronic alternations do not simply involve raising or lowering, but reflect the intervention of further sound changes to produce complex qualitative differences of the sort which OT seems particularly ill-suited to analysing. The alternants might either be seen as independently learned and stored, *contra* the psycholinguistic evidence cited above; or, following Blevins's account of Lardil, they might be 'exiled … to word-formation rules within the morphology proper' (1997: 257), ignoring the interactions of phonology and morphology which are beginning to be understood in models like Lexical Phonology. Alternatively, one might deal with morphological conditioning by reintroducing level ordering into OT, with constraints potentially ranked differently on each level. As we saw in the previous chapter, Bermúdez-Otero (1999) proposes a model of interleaved OT rather than the Strongly Parallel version, essentially to combat difficulties encountered by Sympathy theory in accounting for opaque alternations, and to allow clearer integration of misacquisition as a cause of both opacity and change.

Reranking itself, however, is the main difficulty with Miglio's (1998) analysis, and with similar treatments of sound change within OT. The essential difficulty here is whether the change motivates the constraint reranking, or whether the reranking motivates the change. We might say that if a constraint has visible effects in the phonology, it is necessarily ranked high: so the fact that vowels raise in the Great Vowel Shift is evidence for the relatively high ranking of my constraint (3.18.a), or Miglio's *[-ATR]mm, and the fact that vowels did not raise earlier shows they were then ranked low. Blevins's (1997) description of a constraint as being 'in evidence' at the outset of a sound change first alerted us to this difficulty of ascertaining whether these effects arise because the constraint has been reranked, or whether the reranking takes place in response to a change already going on on the phonetic ground. If the two constraints in (3.18.) reversed their ranking first, then the Great Vowel Shift could be a response to the newly active status of 'vowels are high': but this does not explain the reranking; it presupposes it. On the other hand, if the Great Vowel Shift started for other reasons, and children learning the language ascribed the synchronic results to the previously dormant 'vowels are high' constraint, then the reranking is explained, but not the change. Problems of this kind are familiar from rule-based work, where general, universal tendencies have sometimes unsuccessfully been invoked to account for sound, or indeed syntactic change: this is true, for instance, of the attribution of shifts from OV to VO, as between OE and ModE, to a principle like 'natural serialization' in 1970s discussions of syntactic change. Parallels between this work and the analysis of sound change within OT will be considered in section 3.5 below; but in short, it is impossible to determine sensibly why this principle comes into play precisely when it does, and not otherwise, unless external evidence from parsing, memory limitations and so on is included. If we need reference to non-phonological factors for sound change too, whether those are phonetic or sociolinguistic, then we can still by all means say the result is a reranking of constraints, but calling the reranking explanatory is very problematic.

3.3.3   Historical segment loss

The difficulties identified in Miglio (1998) are by no means unique to that analysis or to the OT treatment of chain shifts: many recur in constraint-based approaches to other sound changes, including segment loss. Indeed, Cho (1995) gives an OT account of diachronic developments in Korean which is rather similar to the Great Vowel Shift case outlined above. Cho allows for the replacement of earlier *nip* 'leaf', which was current until the eighteenth century, by the novel form *ip*, by invoking reranking of the constraint *[ni with Faithfulness. Whereas Faithfulness constraints ideally impose identity between input and output representations, *[ni prohibits the [ni] sequence at the beginning of a prosodic word. When the *[ni constraint, which presumably was earlier too low-ranked to have any discernible effect, came to outrank Faithfulness, the best parse of /nip/ became [ip].

First, Cho's analysis faces the problem of determining appropriate initial representations since, as Sherrard (1997: 83) points out, she tacitly assumes historical constancy of underlying representations, with /nip/ the source for both earlier [nip] and later [ip]; this assumption is at odds with Hutton's (1996) Synchronic Base Hypothesis, which requires the candidates produced by Gen to be based on the synchronically relevant output form, to prevent Old English or Proto-Germanic forms appearing as the underliers for Modern English forms. Cho's work also raises the question of universality. The *[ni constraint looks suspiciously language-specific; and yet, given the assumptions of the theory, it has to be seen as innate, partly because it is based on negative evidence and is therefore unlearnable as it stands, and partly because of its cross-linguistic potential. That is to say, we cannot rule out a possible, parallel future change producing *ip*, *ickel*, *Ixon* and *incompoop* in English, so*[ni must be lurking around innately for English speakers too, just waiting for its chance. Even if we include only those banning constraints actually attested by their presumed effects in particular languages, rather than listing all possible segments and sequences, this will still increase the constraint inventory very significantly in more strongly innatist versions of OT. In addition, if we are to take cross-linguistic evidence seriously in formulating constraints, we can never be sure, since our descriptions of many languages are incomplete, that there is not another language in which Constraint X is 'in evidence': that is, propose a constraint for Korean today, and someone may ascribe effects in Gaelic to it tomorrow. On that basis, my analysis of the Great Vowel Shift has just validated Archangeli and Suzuki's 'vowels are high' constraint for Yokuts.

Here again, we also face the problem of why the reranking happens. If the reranked constraint causes the *ni-* sequence to simplify, why did that constraint come to rank high enough in the eighteenth century to have that effect, when it did not in the seventeenth? Archangeli (1997: 31) tells us that:

Under OT, the formal characterization of language change through time is that constraints are reranked. A prevalent view of diachronic language change is that change occurs when there is imperfect transmission from one generation to the next. Combining these two claims implies that constraints can only be reranked when the evidence for a particular ranking is not very robust.

If this means *ni-* was already on the way out, the reranking is purely a descriptive technique for telling us things were different at two stages of Korean; and any explanation will have to come from outside the theory—in phonetics or acquisition, for instance. The constraints themselves cannot directly explain the change if their order at the time of that change does not predict the output we find, unless we are willing to countenance teleology. In general, OT seems to concentrate on internal explanations, with phonological behaviour constituting a response to the universal constraints. But the violability of these constraints, although beneficial in many ways, introduces tension here: if a change improves harmony, this should be calculated in terms of constraint ordering at the time the development began; but the constraints will subsequently be reranked in response to the change. Why then was the earlier form maximally harmonic then, while the new one is now? This also raises questions for the OT view of language acquisition, which we explored in Chapter 2. If children rank the innate constraints on the basis of language-specific behaviour, discovering the right order to generate the data they hear, sound change presumably will not necessitate reranking for a particular speaker once her grammar is established; instead, reranking is something only the phonologist can discern by comparing the appropriate rankings for the stages before and after the change. However, if the explanation for certain changes lies in the acquisition process, then imperfect learning will have to be a possibility in a constraint-based system. Paradoxically, Tesar and Smolensky's (1998) acquisition algorithm may be too successful here: its results are generally good, but there seems no way of building in imperfect learning, meaning that the capacity for modelling and explaining change in OT is potentially seriously limited.

Restrictions on possible rerankings should also delimit possible sound changes. Since little attention has been paid to change in

OT until relatively recently (perhaps because evidence on prosodic change from earlier language stages is notoriously difficult to interpret, and the strengths of OT lie outside the segmental alternations which have been the focus of most studies of sound change), it is only possible at this stage to provide some questions which might guide further research. Since the power of OT is largely defined by the interaction of constraints, the restrictiveness and the descriptive and predictive power of the model will depend on the provision of answers to these questions (along with other areas requiring further attention, such as the operation of Gen and the incorporation of language-specific phonological rules). For instance, is there a limit on the number of constraints which can be involved in the reranking responsible for a given change? Does reranking to a point high in the hierarchy cause more visible effects, or effects of a predictably different sort, from a change which leaves a constraint still ranked relatively low? Are there particular points in the constraint hierarchy where reranking preferentially occurs?

Although Green (1998) differs in some respects from Cho (1995), he also focuses on reranking in the context of a segment loss, this time the simplification of the [kn] cluster between Middle and Modern English. Green uses this development to illustrate his hypothesis that 'Sound change may be viewed as the promotion of well-formedness constraints towards the top of the hierarchy' (1998: 1), a strategy he refers to as 'the promotion of the Unmarked'. He proposes the constraints and rankings in (3.19.).

(3.19.) DEP-IO   (no epenthesis)

MAX-IO   (no deletion)

IDENT-IO(nasal) (no changing of the feature [nasal])

*σ[kn   (the cluster [kn] is illicit in an onset)

Middle English: DEP-IO ≫ MAX-IO ≫
IDENT-IO(nasal) ≫ *σ[kn

Reranked order: DEP-IO ≫ IDENT-IO(nasal) ≫
*σ[kn ≫ MAX-IO

Reranking promotes *σ[kn, and the result (given the higher-ranking IDENT-IO(nasal), which means the [n] part of the cluster cannot be tampered with) will be loss of the [k]. Green (1998) suggests that input /k/ will also be lost intergenerationally as a result of Lexicon Optimization, a strategy invoked in accounts of acquisition under OT which ensures that selected inputs will be maximally faithful to outputs, as shown in (3.20.). Note that /iafdjskl/ here is just one example of an infinite set of possible inputs of random length and complexity, not obviously related to the output.

(3.20.) 'Possible inputs for the output [noʊ]

a. ☞ /noʊ/   No faithfulness violations

b.   /knoʊ/   One violation of MAX-IO

c.   /iafdjskl/   Multiple violations of MAX-IO and DEP-IO.'

(Green 1998: 2)

The ordering of relevant constraints may also have changed between the reranked version of (3.19.) and the present day. Green suggests that the order of *σ[kn relative to the faithfulness constraints may be gauged by the pronunciation of loans like *Knesset*: if this surfaces as [knɛsət], then *σ[kn must be ranked relatively low, suggesting the order MAX-IO ≫ IDENT-IO(nasal) ≫ DEP-IO ≫ *σ[kn. If, on the other hand, we find [kənɛsət], then *σ[kn demonstrably ranks quite high, supporting MAX-IO ≫ IDENT-IO(nasal) ≫ *σ[kn ≫ DEP-IO.

Green's (1998) interpretation of reranking is certainly preferable to Cho's in its assumption of subsequent alteration of inputs: the old story of virtually constant and unalterable underlying representations characteristic of Chomsky and Halle (1968), which Cho's view approximates, is manifestly at odds with acquisition and with the now-standard notion of a continuum between variation and change. In other respects, however, Green's analysis faces the same problems as the others considered above. Like Miglio (1998), Green proposes rerankings which are neither single nor straightforward. His description of sound change as 'the promotion of the Unmarked' cannot be the whole story, since the relevant well-formedness constraint, *σ[kn, is not the only one reranked: in (3.19.), it is clear that three out of the four constraints in the relevant mini-hierarchy are affected, with *σ[kn and IDENT-IO(nasal) swopping places, but MAX-IO also being demoted. Equally, just as Miglio's account of the Great Vowel Shift involves several rerankings between subshifts, to allow for raising of /a:/ at a later but not an earlier stage of the chain, for instance, so Green (1998) invokes reranking for deletion of [k], and again subsequently to permit the different possible pronunciations of loans in Modern English. For instance, the hierarchy DEP-IO ≫ IDENT-IO(nasal) ≫ *σ[kn ≫ MAX-IO proposed for the deletion stage, is replaced by MAX-IO ≫ IDENT-IO(nasal) ≫ *σ[kn ≫ DEP-IO, where DEP and MAX have changed places, in cases where *Knesset* is pronounced [kənɛsət]: but why did this reranking occur? The obvious answer, because the relevant words surface with inserted schwa rather than deleted or surface [k], is not satisfactory from an explanatory point of view. Green defends his approach, and the analysis of sound change under OT in general, by arguing that 'An OT approach to sound change predicts that the same sorts of sound changes will happen over and over again cross-linguistically, which rule-based approaches to sound change do not' (1998: 2). It would seem, however, that reranking is descriptive at best, fortuitous at worst, and *post hoc* either way, so long as the constraint set is in principle unrestricted, and the reranking itself is not explanatory, but depends in turn on external factors, whether phonetic, functional, or sociolinguistic.

This conclusion is doubly relevant since Green's analysis, like Cho's, includes what is effectively a language-specific constraint in *σ[kn, which may in any case be problematic as an example of the *SEG constraint class criticized by Blevins and Garrett (1998). If we do not wish either to expand the constraint set vastly by including all possible *SEG constraints as innate, and yet wish to retain innate constraints for universally motivated cases, we are faced with a decision. Either such language-specific cases may be formulated as constraints, but taken as learned or invented on the basis of language-specific input data, in which case OT must address the question of how language-specific and innate constraints interact; or another type of formal object must be countenanced, since the language-specific cases will have to be handled by means of language-specific rules. This decision seems to have been taken *de facto* in some OT analyses, since we have already seen that Blevins (1997) and McCarthy (1993) both include rules. The situation is more complex, however, since it is possible to mimic all sorts of characteristics of rule-based phonology in OT even without rules: recall Archangeli and Suzuki's (1997) use of disparate correspondence to effectively write a lowering rule for Yokuts. Schlindwein Schmidt (1996), discussing a vowel-raising chain shift in Basaa, uses just this observation to argue for ordered rules. As she says, 'This is not to say that the candidate evaluation conventions of optimality theory cannot be extended to include globally powerful ones that mimic rule-ordering effects … My analysis of Basaa … simply recognises that one very good way to get rule-ordering effects is to use ordered rules' (1996: 263).

More generally, one might conclude that one very good way to get language-specific phonological effects is to write language-specific phonological rules. These are particularly efficacious in dealing with the synchronic residue of the histories of systems: languages at any particular point in time are dealing with whatever has been bequeathed to them by earlier stages, and not all of this may be streamlined and immediately universally motivable. Accidents of history leave their mark. Naturally, if we need rules as well as constraints, it is incumbent on practitioners of OT to provide a principled division of labour between them. In fact, the root of the problem may be precisely this much-vaunted reduction in OT to a single formal object, rather than the older system of rules and constraints: we pursue this issue, and parallels with other linguistic and non-linguistic theories, in the next chapter.

3.4 OT and variation

As Zubritskaya (1997: 121) notes, 'The examination of sound change in formal phonology has concerned investigation of discrete stages in the historical development of languages.' That is to say, different, sequential grammars are constructed and compared for the periods before and after the change at issue. This approach, however, misses one of the most important insights into language change gained in the twentieth century, namely its profound dependence on variation (Labov 1972; Milroy 1992). Studies of changes in progress, and examination of extragrammatical and specifically sociolinguistic factors, have significantly increased our understanding of the motivation and transmission of sound changes. In the light of these developments, practitioners of formal linguistic theories can take one of two approaches to sound change. They may follow Lightfoot's (1979, 1991*a*, 1999) example, defining language change as the catastrophic, intergenerational discrepancy found between earlier and later grammars, analysed as parameter resetting, or rule change, or constraint reranking, depending on the character and apparatus of the particular model. In such cases, the role of external factors in leading up to a grammatical change is typically recognized, albeit sometimes rather perfunctorily (see 3.5 below), but such factors are explicitly characterized as falling beyond the bounds of the theory itself. Alternatively, linguists may seek to capture the role of external factors in conditioning and promoting change by reflecting them directly in the grammar, for instance by the phonetic grounding of constraints considered above, or in sociolinguistic terms, by introducing a quantitative component, most notably in the shape of variable rules (see Guy 1997*a,b* for discussion).

OT might be expected to fall into the former category: its status as a model operating with completely ranked constraints, each hierarchy converging unambiguously and categorically on a single output for each input form, would seem to preclude the analysis of variation. Variant forms could only emerge in the exceptional case where two candidate parses tie on a pass through constraint evaluation; and the more constraints, constraint types, and additional machinery we find, the less likely we might predict this type of outcome to be: there is almost always likely to be something in the constraint set that will differentiate the two candidates.

In any case, as Anttila (1997: 46) argues, simply factoring in a lack of decision between candidates 'is truly the poor man's way of dealing with variation', since it does not allow frequency effects and differences to be captured. However, the increased attention to change in OT over the last five years or so seems to go along with a greater willingness to confront variation, and a number of solutions, of varying degrees of ingenuity, have been proposed. All involve, in one way or another, the weakening of total ranking of constraints. In standard, earlier versions of OT, constraint hierarchies are seen as totally ordered: that is, for all pairs of constraints R, there is irreflexivity, transitivity, asymmetry and also connectedness, as defined in (3.21.).

(3.21.)   'R is connected if and only if for every two distinct elements x and y in C, $<x, y> \in R$ or $<y, x> \in R$. (Every constraint is ranked with respect to every other constraint.)'

(Anttila and Cho 1998: 36)

Anttila and Cho (1998) argue that the three other properties should be retained, but that connectedness is not a necessary property of properly ranked constraint hierarchies; there is therefore scope for various types of partial ranking. In all these cases, a single partial order will correspond to a set of possible totally ordered tableaux. If a grammar permits more than one ranking, it will generally also permit more than one winning output, and therefore variation is predicted.

These possibilities can best be illustrated by considering two case studies. First, Zubritskaya (1997) explicitly connects variation and change in her analysis of an ongoing development in Russian, namely loss of palatalization assimilation. Her work is based on a very large sociolinguistic survey carried out by the Russian

Language Institute in Moscow, Leningrad and various other cities. The survey is questionnaire-based, and therefore to an extent conservative, but has the advantage of involving a considerable number of informants, so that the results lend themselves to quantitative analysis. Since Zubritskaya is concerned with change, albeit in progress, she naturally invokes reranking; but she stresses that this mechanism is to be evaluated 'for its potential in modeling the actual operation of a change through variation, rather than its advantages in modeling historical changes as a progression of invariant grammars' (1997: 123).

Zubritskaya first introduces the idea of constraint families, each being composed of a series of related constraints defining relative markedness: for instance, the *PLACE hierarchy in (3.22.) tells us, informally speaking, that if any consonant place is to be disfavoured, it will be [pharyngeal], while if only one place is permitted, it will be [coronal]. The members of such subhierarchies are subject to universal, fixed ranking, so that change cannot alter constraints within a family, whether by reranking, reformulation, addition or deletion. Instead, sound change will involve reranking of a single constraint relative to a whole constraint family.

(3.22.) *PLACE: *PHARYNGEAL ≫ *DORSAL ≫ *LABIAL ≫
    *CORONAL

At the start of the twentieth century, Standard Russian had regular palatalization assimilation in consonant clusters; Zubritskaya (1997) ascribes this assimilation to a constraint PAL, which requires [palatal] to be maximally associated. At this stage, she proposes that PAL must have ranked above the constraint family *COMPLEX PLACE shown in (3.23.); however, PAL has subsequently been reranked below *COMPLEX PLACE, with its demotion following a series of steps as it drops below each subconstraint in turn.

(3.23.) *COMPLEX PLACE: *DORS ≫ *LAB ≫ *COR

         | | |

        COR COR COR

The gradual nature of change in progress follows quite naturally from this approach, since a stepwise demotion will predict that different environments will be affected at different stages. However, despite Zubritskaya's earlier declaration that she is concerned with how change arises from variation, she is forced to admit that her model 'describes restructuring of an OT grammar. It neither explains why a sound change operates through variation, nor does it generate the quantitative outcome' (1997: 137). Zubritskaya does not resolve this problem, although she does suggest two possible alternatives: either a grammar competition model might be adopted, allowing co-existing invariant grammars for individual speakers, which then allow the different possible surface variants to emerge; or constraints might be assigned a particular weight, which might change in response to extra-grammatical factors. The mean of a constraint might then drift along a weight scale, competing with other constraints whose weight meanwhile remained constant; this would in a sense build a probabilistic aspect into constraint ranking. However, Zubritskaya's proposals in this last area are extremely schematic and tentative, and cannot yet be evaluated fully.

Anttila (1997), Anttila and Cho (1998), and in particular, Nagy and Reynolds (1997) attempt to capture the quantitative aspect of linguistic variation by a slightly different route, which is frequency-based and, in Anttila's words, involves 'deriving variation from grammar' (1997: 35). The idea here is that each partial ordering will generate a set of tableaux, which in turn will predict a certain set of outputs. If we count the number of times a given output emerges from the total set of possible tableaux, this should predict the relative frequency of the form in actual production.

The question is how this partial ordering is to be achieved. Nagy and Reynolds (1997: 38), in a discussion of end-of-word deletion processes in Faetar, a Francoprovençal dialect spoken in the South of Italy, suggest supplementing the existing mechanisms of OT with 'the notion of a floating constraint, whose hierarchical rankings may change in a principled manner in relation to a certain subset of other constraints whose ranking is fixed, allowing different forms to be optimal under different rankings.'

Nagy and Reynolds (1997) base their analysis on data from 40 speakers of Faetar, who had been asked to name objects and describe the action in pages from a children's picture book, under the impression that they were giving a lesson in Faetar vocabulary. Various reduced forms were produced, following the patterns in (3.24.).

(3.24.) 1. full form

2. no final schwa

3. no final syllable

4. no final syllable or preceding schwa

5. more than schwa + onset + schwa did not surface

e.g.   [brókələ]~[brókəl]~[brókə]~[brok] 'fork'

To account for these patterns, and for the frequency of surfacing forms, Nagy and Reynolds (1997: 43) propose the complex hierarchy of hard-anchored and soft-anchored (or floating) constraints shown in (3.25.).

(3.25.) *AMBI, LX ≈ PR, FILL ≫ *CX COD ≫

$$\left\{ \begin{matrix} \dots\dots\dots\dots \text{ALIGN-PRWD} \dots\dots\dots\dots \\ \left[\begin{matrix} \text{*CODA} \\ \text{*CX ONS} \end{matrix} \right] \gg \text{PARSE} \gg \text{ONS} \gg \left[\begin{matrix} \text{*SCHWA} \\ \text{HNUC} \end{matrix} \right] \end{matrix} \right\}$$

The floating constraints here are ALIGN-PRWD, *CODA and *SCHWA; in total, there are 28 possible rankings, and could therefore be up to 28 optimal candidates, although in fact fewer surface, since some sets of rankings converge on the same outputs. Nagy and Reynolds (1997: 43) see this fact as vitally important, since '... the number of rankings that produce each output form is closely correlated with the number of output forms that occur in the data set.' In the main, the character—and specifically length—of these winning candidates will depend on the relative ranking of PARSE on the one hand, and ALIGN-PRWD and *SCHWA on the other. While PARSE favours the realization of all input material, ALIGN-PRWD (which favours candidates in which the right edge of the prosodic word coincides with the right edge of the main-stressed syllable) and *SCHWA (which disprefers the parsing of unstressed vowels) both in different ways require certain output elements not to surface, where they rank high. Calculations for the variants actually attested in the data can then be compared with those predicted from the number of tableaux giving a particular result, to check the fit: one of Nagy and Reynolds' best cases is given in (3.26.). Here, since eight tableaux select [brokələ], 2 [brok], and 1 each [brokə] and [brokl̩], the predicted output frequencies are 2/3, 1/6, 1/12 and 1/12.

(3.26.) 'fork'	expected	observed
[brokələ]	57	55
[brok]	21	10
[brokə]	11	15
[brokl̩]	11	14

Change in progress, according to Nagy and Reynolds, will therefore involve a floating constraint moving from one end of its domain to the other, again building in gradience.

However attractive this rather integrated picture of variation and change may be, both specific and general difficulties seem inescapable. For every case like that of 'fork' in (3.26.), where the fit between expected and observed frequencies is good (if not perfect: note the disparity for the shortest form, [brok]), there is another where Nagy and Reynolds's (1997) predictions are emphatically not borne out, as shown in (3.27.).

(3.27.)		expected	observed
'spoon'	[kəʌi:ə]	57	40
	[kəʌi:]	43	60
'knife'	[kuttejə]	57	33
	[kuttei]	43	67

In both these cases, the expected pattern is opposite to the one actually found; while in others, forms predicted to occur (like [tawə] 'table', with an expected frequency of 14) do not occur at all. Anttila (1997: 61), reporting similar cases where the wrong quantitative predictions are made, suggests that 'A more fine-grained grammar with more constraints might remedy this short-coming'; but we have already seen that the proliferation of constraints being proposed in OT analyses is potentially prob-lematic in acquisitional terms. Nagy and Reynolds (1997: 49, fn.4) imply that the trend should rather be towards subsuming indi-vidual, and perhaps dubious, constraints under more general schemata, with their statement that

*SCHWA is intended neither as a language-particular constraint nor as a universal constraint against a particular mid-central vowel, but rather as a universal (and violable) constraint on the occurrence of reduced or unstressed vowels.... We might view this as the basis for either a con-straint against unstressed vowels or a constraint in favor of stressed vowels; alternatively, *SCHWA might be seen as having a prosodically more complex basis, requiring, for instance, that all vowels serve as heads of a stress-foot.

This lack of clarity over the constituency of the constraint set also makes it difficult to determine whether there is a fixed set of constraints which are permitted to float: Nagy and Reynolds's (1997: 38) claim that 'rankings may change in a principled man-ner' may only be upheld if so. The model would also be more con-strained if it emerged that some limit can be specified on the distance over which a constraint can float. Nagy and Reynolds also limit their investigation to the shift of a floating constraint from one end of its domain to another, but again, it is not clear whether this limitation is principled, or whether some sound changes might involve extending or reducing that domain while the floating constraint continued to float. Cross-linguistic work on the analysis of different types and examples of sound change, both completed and in progress, would appear to offer the only way of resolving these issues.

Guy (1997*a,b*) points out that a further, unwelcome prolifer-ation of constraints may arise from the practice of 'exploding' sin-gle constraints into families, each member of which may refer to a single feature. This may be necessary in cases where ranking alone cannot give the right results, since the number of times a single constraint is violated is also at issue; and there is no direct way of recognizing multiple violations in OT, since constraints are evaluated against other constraints, not against themselves. Guy supports a variable rule approach rather than an OT picture of variation for precisely this reason. For instance, various factors, including the nature of the preceding segment, affect the likeli-hood of English coronal stop deletion. The generalization here seems to be based on the Obligatory Contour Principle, with deletion being more likely, the more features the preceding seg-ment shares with the focus stop. It is irrelevant which features are shared: what matters is only the number, with effects being equal and cumulative. This is extremely difficult to model under OT: the only possibility would appear to be the division of the OCP into a series of what Guy (1997*a*: 345) calls 'OCP quarks' like OCP-cor, OCP-son, OCP-cont, allowing violations to stack up, but at the familiar rate of one per constraint. However, Guy notes that this makes the wrong predictions, since it implies that these essentially different constraints should be violated at different fre-quencies, and loses the insight that they form a unified set; the fact that they rank together in a cluster also goes unexplained. In addition, 'If OT allows unlimited decomposition of its putatively universal constraints, it will ultimately become so flexible as to be effectively context-free' (Guy 1997*b*: 139), introducing extreme complexity, and perhaps making acquisition impossible.

Incomplete ranking, like imperfect learning, is potentially a serious challenge to language learning under OT in any case. Anttila and Cho (1998: 37) note that the fewer rankings we spe-cify, the more actual tableaux are permissible, but set the problem aside: 'If the constraint set is small ..., one can with little trouble figure out the partial orders hidden in it.' If the constraint set is suffering from galloping inflation, on the other hand, this may not be quite so easy, even if we understood the mechanisms behind the acquisition of partial rankings. Anttila (1997: 48) makes a start here, proposing that children may begin with entirely unranked constraints, which they rank gradually, on the basis of positive evidence; however, some randomness, or lack of ranking, will persist into adult grammars. This does not, however, seem the most realistic way of looking at the situation: surely it is more likely that children will attempt to rank all constraints, producing total rankings for each output form as it is heard. It is, after all, highly improbable that a child will first encounter all the possible variants for a lexical item together; and she cannot know, in advance of hearing those variants, which forms are invariant and which are not. This means that children must be assumed to fully rank their constraints, then subsequently unrank some for forms which they later find to be in variation. This is reminiscent of Archangeli's (1988) picture of learning an underspecified system, where children must be assumed to acquire fully specified input forms, but then strip out many of these values again at a later stage, effectively building in a stage of unlearning.

This view of acquisition might also support a view of competing, fully-ranked grammars, rather than a single grammar per speaker incorporating incomplete ranking, for instance using floating constraints. However, that alternative is not straightforward in learning terms either: Zubritskaya (1997: 142) notes that, 'Although there is no evidence as to how many grammars a speaker may have in his/her head, this model is costly...' For palatalization alone, there are 12 relevant environments, making 2^{12} possible grammars; and loss of palatalization assimilation is only one of the sound changes currently under way in Russian.

All these alternatives, whether they involve complete ranking and competing grammars, partial ranking with floating constraints, or Zubritskaya's (1997) tentative proposal of constraint weighting, also face the problem of the role the grammar plays in variation and change, as opposed to external factors. Anttila (1997: 49) contends that 'It is entirely possible that there exists variation which is not sensitive to style, addressee, gender, age or socioeconomic class, but is completely grammar-driven. To what extent extragrammatical factors are needed in deriving accurate statistics remains an empirical question.' Anttila himself considers a case where internal factors seem paramount, namely the selection of strong and weak allomorphs in the Finnish genitive plural. Although some stems invariably select the strong or weak suffix, others show free variation: this is particularly true of CV-final stems at least three syllables long, as shown in (3.28.).

(3.28.) /naapuri/ 'neighbour'   naa.pu.rei.den ~ naa.pu.ri.en

  /moskeija/ 'mosque'   mos.kei.joi.den ~ mos.kei.jo.jen

However, Anttila's analysis turns out to be disappointingly partial. He leaves open the question of whether allomorphy is involved in these cases, or whether there is a single input form which emerges, for reasons of constraint interaction, as variously strong or weak; and he also sets aside morphophonemic alternations in both suffix and stem (1997: 37):

Many morphophonological intricacies will have to be suppressed to keep this paper to manageable length. Both strong and weak forms have several phonologically distinct realizations: *-iden, -itten, -ten* (strong forms) and *-en, -jen* (weak forms) ... The present discussion is limited to the alternation between the strong and weak classes; I will not address the more specific question of which form within each class is chosen in which environment.... Finally, the stem-vowel alternation *a~o* and *i~e* is triggered by the presence of a following *i, j.* As this does not bear on the main point of this paper, it will be ignored.

The role of extragrammatical as against internal factors is therefore left unclear. In analyses which focus more clearly on actual alternants, however, sociolinguistic factors clearly are relevant to the selection of output forms: Nagy and Reynolds (1997) begin with the hypothesis that speaker's sex, speaker's age, lexical item, following phonological context and pragmatic context may all play a part in determining the surface variant, but find that only age, sex and lexical item are significant. In problematic cases like 'knife' and 'spoon' (see 3.27.), where older speakers conform reasonably well to the predictions of the OT model but younger speakers do not, Nagy and Reynolds must determine the input forms as differing for speakers of different age-groups, in a sense overriding both Gen and Lexicon Optimization. They admit that 'Much work remains to be done to show exactly how to weight the various interacting social factors in order to restrict where constraints float' (Nagy and Reynolds 1997: 48). However, it is extremely unlikely that this approach will ever be predictive, rather than purely responsive to the particular set of social factors and circumstances obtaining in a particular situation. Naturally enough, given the prominent role of contingency in language change, and the deep connection between change and variation, contingency turns out to be highly relevant to variation too. Even in cases like Nagy and Reynolds's 'fork' (see 3.26.), where there is a reasonable match between the predicted and observed variants, the OT analysis itself is not obviously explanatory, as was the case for the OT accounts of change reviewed in the previous section. As Guy (1997b: 138) puts it, the lack of integration of socio-linguistic factors means the formalist OT account

... reduces variation to random selection, and derives specific quantities in the outputs as an epiphenomenon, arising haphazardly from the way the constraint hierarchy determines optimal forms. This result is a sophisticated version of the 'free variation' concept of the structuralists: outputs alternate randomly. As I have noted, that explanation failed when it was shown that variation was not random; this OT version will likely fail for the same reason.

3.5   *Plus ça change*: formal models and language change

3.5.1   *The bigger picture*

The more general question arising from these analyses is whether linguistic change can be modelled, and explained, in formal theories at all. We have already seen that some practitioners of OT claim they can explain changes, but when we look more closely we find reason to doubt those explanations; we might then look a little more sceptically at the theory. But do weaknesses in the OT accounts of variation and change arise from weaknesses in OT, or from a general incompatibility between largely language-specific and contingent processes, and formal, especially universalist, models?

In fact, the theory-internal style of explanation in Optimality Theory is very similar to other formal approaches to language change; in the sections below, I shall compare OT with two approaches to historical syntax, namely Lehmann and Vennemann's ideas about word order going back to the 1970s, and Lightfoot's theories which currently involve parameter resetting, although they have had various earlier incarnations in different generative syntactic models. I use syntactic examples because no parallel tradition exists of a very formal approach to phonological change: either phonological theories have ruled historical evidence out of court altogether (as with some work in Declarative Phonology and Government Phonology; see McMahon (2000) for discussion), or there has been a much greater tendency to invoke external factors. However, OT now seems to be extending into phonology the earlier formalist, top-down approach to change more familiar from syntax, where the theory tells you what you should expect, and the onus is on languages to conform.

3.5.2   *Some formal approaches to syntactic change*

In the next three sections, I shall briefly outline the relevant syntactic models; then identify four actual or potential problems for this sort of approach; and finally assess how these apply to the OT approach to sound change.

The earliest manifestation of a formalist approach to change would appear to involve word order correlations. The universal tendencies illustrated in (3.29.) had first been noted by Greenberg in the 1960s, and his characterization is extremely cautious: occasionally he uses the word 'always', as in Universal 3, but the wording of Universals 2 and 4 is much more typical.

(3.29.) Greenberg (1963):

> Universal 2: In languages with prepositions, the genitive almost always follows the governing noun, while in languages with postpositions, it almost always precedes.
>
> Universal 3: Languages with dominant VSO order are always prepositional.
>
> Universal 4: With overwhelmingly greater than chance frequency, languages with normal SOV order are postpositional.

However, in Lehmann and Vennemann's later work, these word order correlations are distilled down into the two smaller sets shown in (3.30.), with head first across different constructions, or head last. Languages which conform are said to be consistent, and consistency is ascribed to a principle which goes by sundry different names: 'a structural principle of language'; 'the principle of modifier placement' (Lehmann 1973: 48); or 'the principle of natural serialization' (Vennemann 1974: 347). Moreover, if consistency is disrupted, which Vennemann says will always follow from a shift in the basic ordering of V relative to O, then this principle will step in and enforce a realignment of all the other orderings, bringing the language back into the blessed state of consistency, albeit the other way round from where it started.

(3.30.) 1. Head first: VO   Prep.   NG   NA
        2. Head last: OV   Post.   GN   AN

The status of 'natural serialization' is left inexplicit; but more importantly, languages very frequently do not conform—in fact, there are hardly any absolutely consistent languages. Matthews (1981) makes this point by imagining two typological lamp-posts, one representing head-first consistency, the other head-last. The problem is, 'we cannot actually point to any language which is leaning gratefully, even for the odd century or two, against either of our typological lamp-posts. Some are very close to one of them, but not quite there. Others can be seen to stagger purposefully in one direction. Others ... are just swaying about somewhere in the middle' (1981: 10). This means that consistency does not explain change; rather, ongoing change explains lack of consistency—inconsistent languages are in transit. In particular, the initial shift in the order of O and V, which is meant to set the whole subsequent megachange in progress, violates natural serialization, and hence cannot possibly be ascribed to that principle.

In subsequent work, the only way to make sense of particular cases of increasing consistency has involved taking a more functional route. For instance, Hawkins's performance-based approach argues that 'grammars are profoundly shaped by processing' (1994: xi), while Kuno (1974) suggests that centre-embedded structures, which follow from discrepant serialization, seem problematic for our short-term memory: the centre-embedded structure in (3.31.a.) is almost unintelligible, and would be highly likely to be avoided or replaced by a more accessible alternative like the right-embedded one in (3.31.b.), for processing reasons.

(3.31.)   a.   *The cheese [the rat [the cat chased] ate] was rotten.
          b.   The cat chased the rat [that ate the cheese [that was rotten]].

Lightfoot's early work on syntactic change, within the Extended Standard Theory, strongly resembles Lehmann's and Vennemann's, since he proposes a single, not very clearly defined principle, the Transparency Principle. Lightfoot (1979) suggests that opacity or irregularity can build up in a grammar piecemeal, by an accumulation of minor, independent changes. At some specific point, a threshold of tolerable opacity will be crossed, and the earlier analysis will no longer be attainable by language learners, who will instead construct a novel grammar. Evidence for this radical reanalysis is provided by a subsequent set of further changes which it occasions. A brief, schematic example is given in (3.32.).

(3.32.) Lightfoot (1979: 121): '... the Transparency Principle requires derivations to be minimally complex and initial,

underlying structures to be 'close' to their respective surface structures.'
For example, the English modals.

a. The premodals become progressively distanced from
the core set of verbs by a series of independent predisposing changes through Old and Middle English.

b. The limit of tolerable opacity is reached, and children
reanalyse the modals as instances of the new category
M rather than V.

c. This radical reanalysis is manifested by following
changes such as the loss of sequences of modals, the
loss of nonfinite forms of modals, and the limitation of
inversion to modals.

Lightfoot's ultimate goal is to predict where the Transparency
Principle will intervene: or, 'To put it differently, how smart are
language learners? What is the limit to the abstractions that they
postulate?' (1979: 129). However, he makes it quite clear that we
should not expect to predict the particular shape a therapeutic
change will take.

Lightfoot (1991*a*, 1999) are developments of these earlier ideas
within the Principles-and-Parameters model; and in general, this
work comes to focus less and less on Principles and more and
more on Parameters, and specifically on how children set them.
Lightfoot argues that we do ourselves no favours by postulating
parameters which would have to be set on the basis of negative
evidence, or other data inaccessible to language learners: he
makes the strong assumption that children are degree-0 learners,
meaning that only unembedded binding Domains (informally,
main clauses plus a little bit) form part of the triggering experience. When setting parameters, children therefore pay attention
only to 'robust elements which are structurally simple' (1991*a*: ix):
if this were not the case, Lightfoot argues that languages would
not have undergone the changes they have. For instance, he
argues that in Old English, main clause cues to subordinate clause
SOV word order became gradually less readily available, leading

to a parametric resetting, and a reduction of embedded OV order to 66 per cent in 1122, and 11 per cent between 1122 and 1140. In Dutch and German, however, the relevant cues have remained sufficiently robust in main clauses for subordinate OV to persist. If children could equally set parameters on the basis of embedded structure, this difference could not be explained. Nonetheless, this theory is still broadly similar to the 1979 version: predisposing changes build up, eventually causing a new parameter setting, then further changes follow.

However, Lightfoot emphatically does not claim that he is explaining all syntactic changes, arguing that 'Some changes take place while grammars remain constant… Although they do not reflect changes in grammar, such changes nonetheless affect the triggering experience' (1991a: 160). He takes great pains to distance himself from the minor, cumulative changes that set the scene for the parametric change which is his main concern, making it quite clear that these lie necessarily beyond the scope of his model: 'Nonstructural changes do not require and could not receive explanations in terms of a theory of structural parameters. So a theory of grammatical parameters should not seek to explain all the changes that a language might undergo … Many changes … relate to the ways in which grammars are used rather than to their internal structure' (1991a: 166). Instead, these initial changes are attributed to extragrammatical causes, such as borrowing or expressive factors. However, Lightfoot also provides the six diagnostic properties in (3.33.), which are intended to help us decide what sort of change we are dealing with on a particular occasion.

(3.33.) Six diagnostic properties of parametric changes (Lightfoot 1991a):

    1. Simultaneous surface changes

    2. Subsequent chain reactions

    3. Rapidity, and S-curve pattern

    4. Obsolescence follows

5. Involve significant meaning changes

6. Response to changes in unembedded data only.

Lightfoot's ideas can also incorporate the gradual nature of change: although he does propose that grammars change radically, not everyone's grammar will change at once. That is, 'One does not find one set of grammars being replaced by another set overnight; the textual record certainly does not suggest that English speakers had object–verb grammars replaced uniformly by verb–object grammars on some National Head-Change Day in the thirteenth century' (Lightfoot 1999: 107). Arguing for catastrophic or radical change in an internal grammatical sense, or for punctuated equilibrium in the overall pattern of change in a language, therefore is not inconsistent with the sociolinguistic picture of gradual, spreading change: 'It is languages which change gradually: grammars are a different matter' (Lightfoot 1999: 83).

3.5.3   General problems

All these 'top-down' theories of change, which work from the theory to the data and not the other way around, can be seen as having at least potentially four inter-related problems.

a   The non-universality of universals

This issue arises in the context of universal tendencies rather than absolute, exceptionless universals. As Smith (1981: 43) puts it, 'there is no obvious place for a generalization which goes beyond one language but which is not a universal: i.e. something which, *qua* generalization, could be neither learned nor innate.' This is clearly a particular problem for Lehmann and Vennemann's ideas, where natural serialization is meant to be an absolute principle which enforces a shift back to consistency if a language is knocked off course; yet some languages retain inconsistent combinations of properties for centuries. Non-universality is equally a stumbling block for the Transparency Principle.

However, non-universality is resolved in Principles and Parameters, precisely because parametrization gives options, and therefore allows universals to be 'soft'. The cost is that one must be willing to accept a fairly strongly innatist theory. On the other hand, it is not acceptable to invent parameters simply to describe the focus changes: Lightfoot (1999: 215) acknowledges that this does go on, but strongly criticizes the approach of:

a linguist who explains a property of English or a creole language by saying that it manifests some otherwise unmotivated property of Universal Grammar, which in fact makes other grammars unlearnable willy-nilly. This is quite unsatisfactory and is a kind of Lamarckism with a twist: truly acquired properties are given a biological explanation ... There is an increasing tendency to invent properties of UG in order *only* to explain the direction of certain diachronic changes. The fallacy is widespread ...

b   The strength paradox

The next problem, the strength paradox, is the diachronic arm of non-universality. The problem here is with any so-called 'trigger-chain theory', where a principle must be weak enough to allow a change to violate it, like natural serialization when VO becomes OV, but then strong enough to make all the other constructions in the language change in line with the new headedness require-ments. Again, this is a particular challenge for natural serial-ization and the Transparency Principle, but may be relatively unproblematic for Principles and Parameters work on change, because if a parameter has reset between stages x and y, the basis of our calculations has changed in grammatical terms, and the outputs will therefore differ. Of course, this depends on whether the parametric change can be motivated, which is the next poten-tial problem.

c   The chicken and egg problem

Principles and Parameters work on syntactic change seems quite clear-cut if we focus on two distinct stages of the language before and after the change, namely an earlier grammar with parameter setting x, and a later one with setting − x. However, the transition between those stages or grammars raises more questions, partly of historical priority, and partly of causation (which also takes us on to the next issue). The chicken and egg problem, put bluntly, is what comes first? Does a change in the grammar provoke surface changes in response? Or is there some sort of surface change, as a result of which the next population of speakers will inevitably develop a different grammar?

This question simply cannot be resolved by Lehmann and Vennemann (or, indeed, the early Lightfoot): if we are dealing with absolute principles, they should be in evidence all the time. The first time this problem can therefore be confronted seriously is in connection with Lightfoot's later work, where there is some notion of the mechanisms involved in underlying changes in the grammar, typically in the form of parametric resettings. However, Lightfoot's solution may be rather unexpected, since in effect he characterizes resettings as both cause and effect: they are caused by previous changes which lie outside the purview of syntactic theory, and in turn cause further surface changes.

Essentially, Lightfoot's approach involves distinguishing what the theory can or does do from what it cannot or does not. He attempts to separate those surface changes which motivate a change in the grammar, from those later changes which provide evidence of it, and claims, as we have seen, that those two types of change have different causes and characteristics: crucially, the first is outside the remit of Lightfoot's theory, while the second is inside. This depends entirely on the security of the distinction between the prior and subsequent changes (and change types): Lightfoot (1991a) offers the six criteria for decision in (3.33.) above, while Harris and Campbell (1995: 41) contend that 'Lightfoot has no reliable basis for distinguishing the "catastrophic" changes… from the gradually accumulating "environmental" changes' which Lightfoot 'finds relatively uninteresting'. Of course, if one takes an all-or-nothing approach to the explanation of change, and assumes therefore that any theory will fail insofar as it cannot deal with all change of all types, one will be unsympathetic to attempts to categorize changes in this way. On the other hand, those who feel that it is legitimate to draw a line between what changes are contingent and dependent on historical circumstance, from those which may be explicable and perhaps even predictable from inside the bounds of a particular theory, are likely to see this attempt at classification as reasonable in principle, even if preliminary in fact.

d   The external evidence problem

This brings us, finally, to the question of what is meant by explanation. Are all changes explicable theory-internally, or do we have to invoke more performance-based factors for certain types of changes (and can we tell in a reasonable way which types of changes will be susceptible to which type of explanation)? Lehmann and Vennemann fail here, although we have seen that later recastings of natural serialization in functional terms may be more successful. Lightfoot's (1979) Transparency Principle sits uneasily between formal and functional; while Lightfoot (1991*a*, 1999) again suggests that external factors (like contact and expressivity) may be responsible for the motivating changes. Indeed, Lightfoot's ideas on the explanatory scope of his theory seem to have modified over the years: in the early work, we find a clear statement of explanatory intent: 'The aim of this book is to develop a perspective within which one may profitably study how and why the syntax of a language changes in the course of time' (1979: vii). However, on the back cover of his 1999 book, Lightfoot says his model 'is the key to explaining how languages change, and why they change in fits and starts'—but not why languages change. This might suggest that explanation lies ultimately in the changes in the triggering experience, which Lightfoot accepts he cannot deal with at all. If so, this would make the real explanation even of parameter resetting and the subsequent changes a functional matter, and reduce the potential for explanation from internal aspects of the formal theory.

    A diagram showing how the three approaches considered above 'score' in respect of these four problems is presented in

(3.34.). It is clear that Lightfoot's later work does considerably better than the earlier alternatives, although in all three cases, progress in terms of external explanation can only be achieved if functional considerations are incorporated into the model, or if it is accepted that such considerations are relevant and remove explanation of at least some change types from the scope of the formal theory involved.

(3.34.)	L&V	TP	P&P
Non-universality	✗	✗	✓?
Strength	✗	✗	✓
Chicken and egg	✗	✗	✓
External evidence	✓(later)	?	?

3.5.4 Optimality Theory

The next question is how the OT approaches to sound change we have explored in this chapter fare in the face of these four problems. I suggest that, at present, the score stands as shown in (3.35.).

(3.35.)	OT
Non-universality	✓?
Strength	✓
Chicken and egg	✗
External evidence	✗

a   The non-universality of universals

OT very clearly has a solution to the problem of 'soft' universals, because all constraints (at least in principle, and setting aside for the moment the possibility of undominated and inviolable constraints like Orgun's (1996) 'Control' set) are violable. But as with Principles and Parameters, the cost is a very strongly innatist theory. We have already encountered Lightfoot's strong view that parameters should not simply be invented to deal with specific cases of change; but it seems that this is exactly what *is* happening, and to a very considerable extent, for constraints in OT. Cho's (1995) *[ni, Green's (1998) *σ[kn, and Miglio's (1998) *[-ATR]mm are all banning constraints which appear to be invoked fortuitously and *post hoc* to describe the facts of a particular sound change in a particular language; yet the reliance on reranking within OT to account for change means they must be assumed to be innate. This would appear to place most existing analyses of change in OT in a precarious category, since Haspelmath (1999: 5–6) characterizes such specific constraints as 'theoretical constructs that help make the particular analysis work, but that would be the first candidates for elimination if this becomes possible'. Again, we face either extreme constraint inflation, with potentially an innate constraint, which will require ranking during acquisition for every possible segment and sequence, in every possible context; or we require a distinction between universal constraints and language-specific ones (or rules).

b   The strength paradox

Again, it would appear that OT solves this problem just as Principles and Parameters does, by invoking a mechanism of grammatical change which requires the appropriateness or harmony of particular candidates to be calculated differently at different stages, necessitating different surface forms. However, it seems that reranking allows many more options than parameter resetting: changing the setting of a parameter involves only that one parameter, whereas changing the order of constraints involves more than one constraint. Many aspects of the mechanism still remain unclear, as we have seen: for instance, do reranking constraints have to be adjacent? Does reranking to different points in the hierarchy produce predictably different effects? And are there places in the hierarchy where reranking preferentially occurs? There are huge potential problems of limitation and delimitation here.

c   The chicken and egg problem

This also brings us back to the chicken and egg problem. In Green's account of the loss of initial [k], does this phonological effect arise because the constraints have been reranked, or is the reranking a response to an ongoing change? If the reranking comes first, then the loss of [k] could be a response to the newly active status of 'no initial [kn-]', but that does not explain the reranking; rather, it presupposes it. On the other hand, if the change started for other reasons, and learners ascribed the synchronic results to the previously dormant constraint, this explains the reranking, but not the change.

This problem seems significantly worse for OT than for Lightfoot's parametric approach, principally because Lightfoot distinguishes the motivation for the new parameter setting (that is, the initial set of predisposing changes due to borrowing or other external factors) from the later ones which follow from the grammatical change and give evidence for it. In OT, however, the motivation and the evidence for the constraint reranking are precisely the same, namely the change we are trying to explain in the first place. In Green's analysis, for instance, the only relevant issue is that [kn-] surfaces at one stage, but only [n-] at the next. Reranking only serves to formalize the same facts differently for a later group of speakers; there is no further, later evidence for the reranking itself apart from, again, the focus change. This is description rather than explanation.

d   External evidence

The previous issue overlaps with external evidence, and the question of what can in principle be explained within a particular model. Again, there is, at this stage, a fundamental difference between the OT and parametric approaches. Lightfoot says the changes with external, functional causes explain the parametric change, so the space for explanation in the theory itself is arguably becoming more and more limited. In OT, there is a move in some quarters towards considering some of the constraints themselves as functionally motivated (see Hayes 1996; Haspelmath 1999); but this typically goes along with a reduction or rejection of the innateness of constraints, which could compromise some of the OT solutions to other problems suggested above. In mainstream, strongly innatist versions of OT, explanations of change are still quite clearly intended to be theory-internal (see 3.3 above). And there are currently very few attempts to draw a line between what we can do in the theory and what we should not expect to, in the way Lightfoot suggests.

The comparisons above do not tell us that all formal theories have the same problems when it comes to analysing change, but do show that it can be useful to evaluate them along similar lines to see where progress is being made, or where, conversely, earlier solutions are being lost and we are effectively going backwards. OT seems at present to be falling into the old Standard Generative trap of seeing description and explanation as interchangeable concepts. It is essential that we bear this danger in mind, as well as the possibility of intrinsic limitations on internal explanation: as Faarlund (1990: 60–1) tells us, 'If we never depart from the domain under study to find explanations, we end up with a circular system where pure formalisms become explanations.' Real, valid explanations from within a theory are more likely to be accepted and applauded if they are not included in a rag-bag category with *ad hoc* descriptions stated in terms of the same mechanisms. As we shall see in more detail in the next chapter, recognizing cases where external factors come into play and where historical contingency and truly descriptive mechanisms may need to be invoked, is therefore not a weakness, but potentially a strength.

4

Cognates and Comparisons: Natural Morphology and Neo-Darwinian Evolutionary Biology

4.1 A problem shared

At present, some of the arguments around OT are uncannily—and uncomfortably—like those current in the early days of Standard Generative Phonology: the definition of abstractness may differ, and we face an accumulation of constraints rather than rules, but the fundamental problems are very similar. Furthermore, they might be seen as arising from a shared conceptual weakness, in the form of a lack of constraint on the main formal mechanism of the theory, namely rules for Standard Generative Phonology and constraints for OT. Because of the drive inherent in both models to derive all phonological phenomena from a single mode of analysis, the rules and constraints become more and more divorced from actual data, and themselves become the focus of attention. One possible way forward for OT has emerged from the last two chapters: we might argue that restrictions on the number, type and language-specificity of constraints are necessary, propose new machinery, and suggest restrictions in turn on that, ideally ensuring at each stage that we understand the interaction of the new mechanisms with those already established in the theory, and that we do not simply allow a proliferation of ill-understood and situation-specific tools.

In this chapter, I propose to tackle some of the problems of OT at a more theoretical level. Let us accept for the moment that, given the (only partially understood) power of Gen and the lack of limitation on new constraints, it is probably possible to provide an analysis of any phonological phenomenon in a fairly orthodox version of OT, lacking language-specific rules, though almost certainly including some additional machinery in the form of OO-Correspondence, Sympathy and the like. Why, however, should we wish to collapse all phonological phenomena into one set in this way, ascribing them uniquely to universal constraints? I shall show that, when we consider other models inside and outside of linguistics, we find an expectation that we should *not* be able to manage with just a single kind of formal statement; instead, we should anticipate needing system-specific and universal mechanisms. In fact, if we accept both constraints and rules but work to divide them appropriately, phonological theory might be in a better position to deal with both universal and specific behaviour than either of our comparand systems, which recognize the necessity of operating at both universal and system-specific levels, but do not always have dedicated mechanisms for doing so. Following from the previous chapter, it should come as no surprise that both models considered here derive these insights on the necessity of system-specific tools very largely from the analysis of history and change, and the inevitable incursion of contingency.

4.2   Natural Morphology

Prince and Smolensky (1993: 2), acknowledging various influences on their work and identifying models sharing similarities with OT, point out that 'The work of Stampe … , though framed in a very different way, shares central abstract commitments with our own.' Natural Phonology (Stampe 1972; Donegan 1993) introduced an idea of phonological naturalness based on markedness: unmarked features and processes were seen as genetically determined, while marked ones, which are defined as straining the human language capacity, may arise through linguistic change.

Children learning a language must then suppress the innate, natural processes in language-specific contexts, and learn morphophonological rules, which reflect past sound changes in that system. There are some clear parallels with OT here—and perhaps further connections in that Natural Phonology faced strong criticism for not sufficiently defining naturalness, and for proposing as innate 'laws' which were in fact extremely specific. However, Natural Phonology did give rise to a related model, Natural Morphology, in which these issues are more fully addressed.

Natural Morphology (Dressler 1985; Dressler *et al.* 1987; Wurzel 1989) is a good comparand for OT in that it is a theory of preferences explicitly dealing with markedness (which it essentially equates with naturalness). OT is also strongly markedness-based: for instance, Prince and Smolensky (1993: 188) adopt markedness theory at the expense of underspecification; and because OT constraints are violable, they similarly encode preferences. As we shall see, however, the two models also diverge in ways which might be illuminating for OT.

Natural Morphology identifies certain morphological forms and constructions as natural, or unmarked, on the basis that they occur frequently cross-linguistically; appear often and in numerous contexts in languages where they occur; are relatively resistant to change but often result from changes; occur in pidgins and are introduced early in creoles; and are acquired early by children, but unaffected or lost late in aphasia. Borrowings and neologisms typically gravitate towards the unmarked pattern, as do marked forms when affected by speech errors. Factors underlying naturalness are then identified.

First, there is a meta-level of three universal principles: constructional iconicity (whereby 'more' meaning corresponds to 'more' form); uniformity (whereby a single meaning is consistently realized by the same affix or process); and transparency (whereby a given affix or process consistently realizes a single meaning). There are tentative suggestions that certain morphological phenomena may be ruled out by conflicting with all three criteria, and Dressler (1985: 326) sees one goal of Natural

Morphology as providing 'negative predictions, i.e. definitions of conceivable morphological phenomena which are too unnatural to occur in languages of the world'. In general, however, Natural Morphology is a theory of preferences rather than absolute prohibitions, and more attention is paid to the very frequent cases where relatively unnatural phenomena arise.

It is important to note that explanation in Natural Morphology is not intended to be internal to the theory, or indeed to the morphology. Instead, the three major principles are seen as having their motivation in neurobiology, for instance relating to perception, processing, or memory limitations. We see here the results of earlier work on historical syntax and morphology. A great deal of ink was spilt in the 1970s, as we saw in the last chapter, on putative changes from head–modifier to modifier–head order cross-linguistically: recall Lehmann's (1973: 48) 'structural principle of language', or 'principle of modifier placement', and Vennemann's (1974) 'principle of natural serialization'. There are three major problems with natural serialization and the like. First, although the principle allows for the realigning of constituent order across constructions once an initial change has knocked the system off balance, there is no explanation for that initial change. Second, commentators at the time found numerous cases where languages have persisted for centuries with mixed modifier–head and head–modifier order with no apparent inclination towards change. Finally, the status of the principle(s) involved was unclear: making natural serialization innate only pushed the explanation back one step, and still left exceptions as problematic; but if the principle was not innate, what was it based on? Only when perceptual factors, for instance, were brought into play in this discussion did some of these issues become clearer (Kuno 1974; Vincent 1976). If centre-embedding, for instance, causes perceptual problems, and if consistent head–modifier ordering or the reverse reduces the likelihood of centre-embedding, then we can begin to understand both why a certain degree of consistency is preferred, and why violations of consistency can be apparently without consequence in one system (where presumably the threshold for parsing difficulties has not been crossed), but lead to wholesale change in another. The key seems to be to regard principles as defeasible; to look for ultimate explanation outside the theory, and even outside the subcomponent of linguistics under consideration; and to pay attention to the role of language change.

All of these lessons are taken to heart in Natural Morphology. The three universal principles are seen as violable (although as we have seen, morphological forms conflicting with all of them might be expected not to occur), and are motivated by universal and typically neurolinguistic considerations; Dressler *et al.* (1987: 11) refer to 'the extralinguistic foundations of linguistic...naturalness.' More explicitly, Dressler (1985: 322), in what would also be an admirable summary of our conclusions from the natural serialization debate, states that 'universals...are not somewhere in the air or simply inherited in the genetic code, but they are based on the exigencies and functions of universal performance'; and consequently, 'these universals have the function of serving performance in communication and cognition.'

The theory also includes a strong claim that 'language change always proceeds in the direction of naturalness' (Wurzel 1989: 17). However, relatively unnatural morphological phenomena may also develop. In part, these reflect conflicts among the principles, following from tensions between production and perception, or sociocommunicational trade-offs between speaker and hearer; so, transparency may allow optimal decoding, but taken to the utmost, would produce extreme agglutination and words of vastly more than optimal length. Mayerthaler (1988) even gives a hierarchy, albeit a tentative one, showing the priority given to each principle, suggesting that naturalness in terms of uniformity and transparency outranks constructional iconicity, which in turn outranks phonetic iconicity. Unnatural morphology may also reflect the fact that naturalness in phonology is calculated on different bases from morphology, and change in the two will therefore follow conflicting agendas. Hence, natural sound changes may shorten words, causing morphological difficulties. The Proto-Germanic nominative plural of 'drop' was *drupan-ir, which was progressively reduced to *drupan in Proto-Norse, and *drupa* in Old Swedish. Although this was presumably easier to pronounce, *drupa* was also the genitive, dative and accusative singular, and the genitive and accusative plural: hardly optimal symbolization of morphological categories. Later in Swedish, a form *drupar*, peculiar to the nominative plural, developed; but in casual speech and certain dialects, the [r] is again dropping (Wurzel 1989). Such conflicts are taken to drive change, and lead to mixtures of relatively natural and relatively unnatural morphological (and phonological) features.

However, Natural Morphology does not restrict itself to such universal or system-independent naturalness, but also includes system-dependent or language-specific markedness measures. Within a language, larger classes are taken to be dominant, and there are various system-defining structural properties which define normal morphological behaviour for a given language. For instance, languages may have base-form or stem inflection, neither of which is in universal terms more natural than the other, and in a mixed system, change towards one pole may be driven by considerations of frequency in that system. In German, base-form inflection is the norm, and consequently stem inflected plurals like *die Firma–die Firmen* 'business' are undergoing reinterpretation to the base-form type, giving *die Firma–die Firmas* (Wurzel 1989). Furthermore, when system-defining structural properties conflict with the universal principles, the language-specific type appear to take precedence. In pluralization, stem and base-form suffixation are of equivalent naturalness, so the change described above for German is neutral with respect to universal considerations. However, any type of suffixation will be preferred to stem modification on the grounds of constructional iconicity, and we might therefore expect a further change in German, from umlaut to suffixed plurals. This is exactly what we find in the case of neuter nouns, with *das Boot* 'boat' replacing its earlier plural *die Böte* with novel *die Boote*. But in masculines precisely the opposite development seems to be occurring, with *der Hund* 'dog', *der Strand* 'beach' developing new umlaut plurals *die Hünde*, *die Strände.* Wurzel (1989) ascribes this counter-iconic change to the greater frequency of umlaut plurals in German masculine nouns: that is, system-defining structural properties of this kind, even holding over subclasses of forms defined by, say, gender, can outweigh universal properties in determining the course of linguistic change. Since system-specific structural properties can themselves change over time, typically as a result of sound change, we again see a complex interaction of universals with language-specific factors, both synchronic and diachronic, in shaping linguistic systems.

Natural Morphology, like Optimality Theory, is therefore based around a set of defeasible constraints. Although in Natural Morphology all determinants of naturalness ultimately reflect the needs of production, perception and acquisition, these are explicitly divided into two categories, defined at a universal or a language-specific level. Universal principles still encode preferences, but are by definition not themselves subject to change, whereas the system-defining structural properties characterizing a particular system are liable to alteration across time. Both types, however, are instrumental in determining the course of change in a particular language. Despite the central role diachrony assumes in Natural Morphology, it is recognized that historical developments themselves are not always amenable to theory-internal explanation: Dressler (1985: 325) accepts that

no account of English morphology within Natural Morphology may neglect the two historical accidents, that (1) medieval English had a fairly inflecting morphology, but underwent drastic phonological change..., (2) that it was subject to massive Latinate influence in the lexicon and morphology, i.e. Natural Morphology has nothing to say about the Battle of Hastings.

In effect, then, Natural Morphology recognizes the need for three levels of statements. First, there is a universal set of principles; we might recognize a parallel here with the class of undominated constraints in OT. Both at present are theoretically seen as violable, but this causes uneasiness for both models. Thus, we have seen proposals in Natural Morphology to rule out universally prohibited morphological structures by interaction of the three overarching principles, although this idea is not fully developed; while in OT, the very fact that certain constraints remain universally undominated means they are *de facto* inviolable, a fact remaining unexplored in the current model. One way or another, we see here tentative reference to a class of absolute universals, and to the necessity of ruling out variation which would take us beyond the bounds of natural language, however this is to be achieved. Secondly, Natural Morphology involves system-specific structural properties, effectively parametrized definitions of the morphological systems of particular languages which allow specification of the types of marker, type of inflection, degree of syncretism, and morphological categories marked. These share strong affinities with the bulk of the constraints in OT, which are rankable and truly violable. The main differences would appear to be the priority of system-specific properties over universal principles in Natural Morphology, whereas in OT the undominated constraints by definition outrank the others; and the explicit derivation of both sets of statements in Natural Morphology from 'the exigencies and functions of universal performance' (Dressler 1985: 322). In OT, phonological data are seen as responses to the constraints, and the rationale for the constraints themselves is frequently not discussed (and we have seen the difficulties presented by proposing an innate principle without identifying a rationale for it in the case of natural serialization). Where constraints in OT *are* seen as grounded, they are often not considered to be innate (Hayes 1996; Haspelmath 1999). Finally, Natural Morphology recognizes historical accidents, which shape systems but which are outside the remit of the theory. These accidents can arise internally, because of changes in another component of the grammar, or externally, by some aspect of speaker behaviour resulting, for instance, from language contact: either way, we are dealing with interactions of a language system with its environment, and with resultant language-specific behaviour which is not predictable, but only describable. We turn now to a further comparison of OT with the archetypal theory dealing with the interaction of systems and environments, namely evolutionary biology.

4.3   Neo-Darwinian evolutionary biology

Evolutionary biology attempts to explain how current (and past, now extinct) species have diversified from an original common source. Darwin (1859, reprinted 1996) began with the Malthusian hypothesis that population growth will eventually be checked, so that not all organisms will have surviving offspring; the question then is to identify the factors determining which organisms will be successful in this reproductive sense, and which will not. Darwin's contribution was the idea that, if some variant was beneficial to the organisms manifesting it in their particular environment, then it would confer some reproductive advantage. Moreover, however tiny this apparent advantage might be, it would become amplified over time provided it could be inherited, since offspring characteristically resemble their parents more than other randomly chosen members of the same population. Dennett (1995: 68) calls this the Principle of the Accumulation of Design, since it enables the development of extremely complex biological structures over long periods of time, without requiring some Higher Intelligence to do any actual designing. The only piece missing from this Darwinian jigsaw puzzle is the unit of heredity itself. Darwin proposed rather sketchily that offspring would inherit a mixture of parental features; the subsequent combination of his ideas with those of Mendel, who had earlier suggested the gene and the first principles of genetic inheritance, but whose work Darwin had not encountered, led to the so-called neo-Darwinian synthesis of the first half of this century. Mutation at the genetic level, which will be inherited according to relatively well-understood mathematical laws depending on the nature of the heritable trait and its presence in one or both parents, will then lead to variation in the population; this in turn is susceptible to natural selection, depending on any benefit (or the reverse) which the particular variant may give rise to in the environment concerned; and beneficial variants may then become strongly numerically dominant, and increasingly complex, over time. If enough of these distinguishing features develop, and particularly when geographical distance also plays a part, then populations may diverge and ultimately speciation will occur.

Given mechanisms of this sort for incorporating changes into organisms, and for preferring some to others, the inevitable next step is to consider possible constraints: in other words, we turn to questions of biological possibility and plausibility, and what determines this. Again, we seem to be dealing with three levels of explanation: a superordinate set of absolute constraints which arise from the laws of physics and mathematics; a class of violable constraints; and a final series of species-specific descriptions.

Let us begin with what, following D'Arcy Thompson (1917), we might call the laws of growth and form. As Gould (1991: 171) puts it, 'however much we celebrate diversity and revel in the peculiarities of animals, we must also acknowledge a striking "lawfulness" in the basic design of organisms. This regularity is most strongly evident in the correlation of size and shape.' Such correlations are encoded in the so-called scaling laws, illustrated in (4.1.), which shows the skeletons of two extinct animals, *Neohipparion* on the left and *Mastodon* on the right.

(4.1.) *Neohipparion* and *Mastodon*: redrawn after Schmidt-Nielsen (1972: 88).

It is immediately obvious, although the skeletons are drawn to the same size, that these animals must have been very different: the *Mastodon* would have been slow-moving, and is assumed to have been roughly elephant-sized, while the more gracile *Neohipparion*, in fact an extinct ancestor of the horse, was the size of a deer. Our intuitions here reflect the operation of physical laws: essentially, because volume increases as the cube of length, while surface area increases as the square of length, smaller animals have proportionally a much greater surface area than larger ones. Conversely, the greater proportional volume of large animals means they need disproportionately large, thick bones to support them, since the cross-section of their bones must increase beyond linear scaling. Large animals therefore share certain immediately obvious physical characteristics, being relatively short and heavy-boned.

Various other characteristics of relatively large animals can be seen as direct responses to these physical restrictions; for example, internal organs will develop, with the lungs acting as surrogate extra surface area for gas exchange, and a circulation system will be required because direct diffusion cannot reach all parts of a large organism. Tapeworms, as much simpler creatures, can be 20 feet long, but cannot be more than a fraction of an inch thick, since food and oxygen have to be able to permeate the whole organism directly. Any change in thickness would require extremely radical internal development (Gould 1991). Further consequences involve metabolic rate: as Schmidt-Nielsen (1972: 92) points out,

... if a steer is designed with the metabolic rate of a mouse, to dissipate heat at the rate it is produced, its surface temperature would have to be well above the boiling point. Conversely, if a mouse is designed with the weight-related metabolic rate of a steer, to keep warm it would need to have as surface insulation a fur at least 20cm thick.

From the relation of volume and surface area, then, we can derive exceptionless generalizations in biology, and specify certain limits on organisms: for instance, because of skeletal scaling, there could be no land animal the size of a blue whale, while the limits of gas exchange mean no single-celled motile animal could be the size of a human. Further biological features, such as metabolic rate, can be related to basic attributes of length, volume and body mass. To take an example, kinetic energy increases as length to the power 5, so if a child half the height of an adult falls over, his head will hit the floor with only 1/32 the energy of a falling adult; similarly, when hitting another child, he will be able to summon up only 1/32 of adult energy (Gould 1991: 175). However, underlying the scaling relations are typically power laws based on quarters: the metabolic rates of organisms scale as three-quarters body mass; rates of cellular metabolism, heartbeat, and maximal population growth scale as minus one quarter body mass; and times of blood circulation, embryonic growth and development, and life-span scale as one quarter body mass (West, Brown and Enquist 1997). Although quarter-power scaling applies across animals, plants and microbes, and encompasses an unexpectedly diverse range of biological phenomena, there has up to now been no general theory explaining the power laws. West, Brown and Enquist (1997), however, attempt to derive them from a model of the transport of essential materials through linear networks, which they assume to branch in a fractal pattern; their results make predictions consistent with data from mammalian circulatory systems, and remain to be tested on plant vascular systems, and insect tracheal tubes, which should be amenable to similar modelling if the theory of general fractal configuration is correct. What is interesting for us here is the fact that the identification of absolute laws is not seen as the final step: explanation is pursued further, in an attempted unification of these universals, an exploration of the factors underlying them, and ideally the eventual discovery of motivations, which may involve recourse to external factors like gravity or the laws of physics, or may, as in the case of the power laws, reflect the exigencies of biological performance.

However, evolutionary theorists would not get very far by considering only these exceptionless laws: there is a further class of general tendencies which may be violated in particular circumstances. Perhaps the best-known example is the cross-species correlation of brain size and body weight. At first sight, we might seem to be dealing here with another power law, since brain size appears to increase regularly at two-thirds the rate of body weight. However, if we plot expected brain size on this basis, we find that all primates are above the expected curve for mammals, with *homo sapiens* the furthest removed from the norm (Gould 1991, Ch.22). Pilbeam and Gould (1974) plotted cranial capacity against inferred body weight for *Australopithecus africanus*, and found that modern *homo sapiens* has a brain three times bigger, an increase which they found could not be ascribed to increased body size alone. Jerison (1973), working with a wide range of fossil data, hypothesizes that brain size can also reflect particular ways of life. Jerison identified an expected encephalization quotient per species, where a level of 1 would indicate exactly the expected two-thirds relation between brain and body size, less than 1 would show a smaller than expected brain, and more than 1, a larger than expected brain. He then plotted carnivores against ungulate herbivores, their probable prey, for four periods from the Early Tertiary, approximately 70 million years Before Present, to modern times. Jerison found that the carnivores had consistently larger brains, presumably reflecting the fact that they needed to outwit and outrun their prey; however, the brains of herbivores also showed a consistent size increase over time, perhaps reflecting what Dawkins (1986: 178) calls an 'arms race' between species. In a test case, Jerison compared the cranial capacities of South American animals at a period when this area was an island lacking placental carnivores. The marsupial carnivores filling the equivalent biological niche showed low encephalization quotients, and the herbivores, as might be expected in the circumstances, failed to show an increase in brain size. They also, as Gould (1991) observes, vanished extremely quickly after the Isthmus of Panama rose and advanced carnivores crossed from North America. Interestingly, Jerison also tested the most ancient brain cast known of a primate, the 55 million year old *Tetonius homunculus*, and found an encephalization quotient which he assesses as three times as large as an average mammal of that time. The relatively large primate brains found today, with *homo sapiens* forming the limit of that range, therefore reflect and continue an extremely early development in primates.

Although the exceptionless laws controlling factors like skeletal scaling lie outside the purview of natural selection, rather determining the boundaries of possible biological diversity, violable constraints of the type governing the relation between brain size and body weight do not. In cases of this sort, a particular, base pattern might be established (such as Jerison's encephalization quotient of 1), but interactions of organism and environment will give rise to variation (such as the larger brains of early primates). If variants are beneficial, as Jerison hypothesized larger brains would be to predators, then these traits will be amplified and developed, producing greater than expected increases in size, and exerting selective pressure on prey species to keep up. Recall that natural selection determines reproductive success: a slow, small-brained herbivore consumed in infancy will not be leaving descendants.

We have now introduced a further consideration relevant to these defeasible biological constraints: if biologists find excursions from the norm, they attempt to find reasons, typically regarding the resulting trait as constituting an adaptation which allows the organism to do a particular job, or to do it better than before. Thus, carnivores evolve bigger brains to maintain an advantage over their prey; mammals in Australia, South America and the New World have all developed so as to produce 'a specialist for each trade' (Dawkins 1986: 102), which come to resemble the fellow specialists in the other geographical areas; and because herbivores tend to run, and to do so on the tips of their toes, their nails have evolved into hooves. The natural tendency of the evolutionary biologist when confronted with some trait is therefore to ask why it has evolved, and in what sense it constitutes an adaptation.

However, as Dawkins (1995: 112) rather exasperatedly notes,

We humans have purpose on the brain. We find it hard to look at anything without wondering what it is "for", what the motive for it is, or the

purpose behind it. When the obsession with purpose becomes patho-
logical it is called paranoia ... But this is just an exaggerated form of a
nearly universal delusion.

Dennett (1995: 212–13) makes a comparison with reverse engineering, whereby an engineer interested in how a rival's product
works will take it to bits and try to figure out the function of all
the components:

Of course, if the wisdom of the reverse engineers includes a healthy
helping of self-knowledge, they will recognize that this default assumption of optimality is too strong: sometimes engineers put stupid, pointless things in their designs, sometimes they forget to remove things that
no longer have a function, sometimes they overlook retrospectively
obvious shortcuts.

Because natural selection has to make modifications of structures that are already present, so that evolution never begins with
a completely clear slate, this kind of patchwork appearance is not
always incompatible with an adaptationist viewpoint. In other
words, natural selection is like an architect starting with an existing building, recycling bedrooms as bathrooms, extending poky
kitchenettes, and adding extra floors: the result might not be as
streamlined as a new-build project on a green-field site; it might
even be more interesting; but the output of both processes is still
a house, with the usual functions of a house. Although our constraints, the mechanism of natural selection, and the assumption
of adaptation can explain many traits, there will be some which
cannot sensibly be regarded as adaptations. We face here the
problem of system-specific description and historical accident
familiar from Natural Morphology and, indeed, from OT.

Gould and Lewontin (1979: 587) cite the information notice on
a fibreglass *Tyrannosaurus* in the Boston Museum of Science,
which reads: 'Front legs a puzzle: how *Tyrannosaurus* used its tiny
front legs is a scientific puzzle; they were too short even to reach
the mouth. They may have been used to help the animal rise
from a lying position.' This assessment illustrates precisely the

obsession with purpose identified above: we notice a particular characteristic of a species, and attempt to reverse engineer its function. Moreover, we assume that 'each trait plays its part and must be as it is' (Gould and Lewontin 1979: 585). In cases where a trait seems to function suboptimally, 'interaction is acknowledged via the dictum that an organism cannot optimize each part without imposing expenses on others' (ibid.) Gould and Lewontin accuse adaptationists of recognizing mechanisms other than natural selection and adaptation, such as genetic drift, but of either circumscribing them so radically that they are of no effective use, or of simply ignoring the alternatives in practice, opting preferentially for a plausible-sounding adaptive explanation without testing or discussion. Moreover, they argue that the adaptationist programme is too flexible, and allows too many possibilities, permitting adaptationists to follow three rules of thumb which in fact seriously impede progress: 'If one adaptive argument fails, try another … If one adaptive argument fails, assume that another must exist; a weaker version of the first argument … In the absence of a good adaptive argument in the first place, attribute failure to imperfect understanding of where an organism lives and what it does' (Gould and Lewontin 1979: 586).

Gould and Lewontin argue that we must also recognize non-adaptive traits, which they introduce using an architectural analogy. In the church of San Marco in Venice, the fact that the dome is mounted on a series of rounded arches creates a series of tapering triangular spaces, known as spandrels. 'Each spandrel contains a design admirably fitted into its tapering space. An evangelist sits in the upper part flanked by the heavenly cities. Below, a man representing one of the four Biblical rivers … pours water from a pitcher into the narrowing space below his feet' (1979: 581–2). Gould and Lewontin argue that, because the mosaics fit so beautifully into the spaces, we are tempted, in adaptationist mode, to assume that the spandrels were designed for the mosaics, instead of resulting from the constraints of the architectural design and being happily turned to good use by the artists. We see here the process of exaptation (also recognized for language by Lass 1990), whereby a feature which has lost its original purpose, or which arose as a by-product of something else, is recycled; such biological recycling may be a long-term undertaking and be subject to natural selection. That is, 'putting a dome on top of four arches gives you a spandrel, but it does not give you a mosaic depicting an evangelist and a man pouring water out of a pitcher ... To get the actual mosaic you need a designer. The designer corresponds to natural selection' (Pinker and Bloom 1990: 710).

Regardless of this subsequent role of natural selection, the spandrel example establishes the existence of characteristics whose initial existence is not directly adaptive. Such non-adaptive traits seem to fall into two classes: some are by-products of other characteristics, which may themselves be truly adaptive; others are simply historical accidents. The short front legs of Gould and Lewontin's *Tyrannosaurus* may belong in the first category, reflecting an automatic consequence of an increase in head and hindlimb size occasioned in turn by the species beginning to walk upright (Gould and Lewontin 1979: 144). Many aspects of the human body plan reflect the history of our species, and not all are maximally convenient: childbirth is difficult for *homo sapiens* because the exigencies of walking upright have certain consequences for the anatomy of the pelvic area, and human babies therefore have to be born relatively underdeveloped, to enable their heads to pass down the birth canal. More specifically, it is adaptive for bones to be hard, and one way of achieving this is to make them out of calcium, which happens to be white; but this does not mean that the whiteness of bones is directly amenable to adaptationist explanation. The structure of haemoglobin, a necessary molecule in transporting oxygen around the body, determines the redness of blood, which is in itself neither adaptive nor necessary, since lobsters, for instance, have green blood.

We see here an overlap with the second category of non-adaptive traits, which are conditioned and circumscribed by their history. Thus, many current animals have four legs, simply because the first vertebrate to crawl out of the sea was a tetrapod. That need not have been the case, but was, in this particular world.

Structures which could be otherwise are extremely common in biological species, and even proposing interacting constraints and taking account of the environment cannot always allow us to fully understand them. Even if a trait is adaptive, this does not always mean we can predict the precise shape and character it has. Dennett (1995: 123) quotes George Williams (1985: 20) who, in confessional mode, admits:

I once insisted that " ... the laws of physical science plus natural selection can furnish a complete explanation for any biological phenomenon." ... I wish now I had taken a less extreme view and merely identified natural selection as the only theory that a biologist needs in addition to those of the physical scientist. Both the biologist and the physical scientist need to reckon with historical legacies to explain any real-world phenomenon.

Constraints and general mechanisms, then, can help us delimit what is possible, but to understand actual organisms or genomes, 'we have to turn to the historical process that created them, in all its grubby particularity' (Dennett 1995: 129). Different species or groups within a species may simply develop different solutions to the same fundamental problem, for instance. Gould and Lewontin discuss the West Indian land snail *Cerion*: snail populations on windy, exposed coasts almost always have white, thick, squat shells, but different developmental pathways converge on the whiteness, thickness and squatness. All these characteristics are indeed adaptive, but 'would it be fruitful to ask why—in the sense of optimal design rather than historical contingency— *Cerion* from eastern Long Island evolved one solution, and *Cerion* from Acklins Island another?' (1979: 150). The elephant and the rhinoceros have broadly similar body-plans, arising from the influence of the universal scaling laws, and live in broadly similar environments: but in only one case has the ancestral nose developed into a trunk. More generally, the fauna of Australia and Africa are strongly resemblant. The environment is open savannah in both cases, the climates are similar, and certain species fill equivalent niches: we might say that the Tasmanian 'wolf',

Thylacinus, corresponds to the jackal. However, mammals in Australia are predominantly marsupial, while those of Africa are placental. Such major regularities might look as though they ought to reflect constraints directly, but history mediates in unpredictable ways: 'There used to be two or more ways this problem might be solved, but now that some ancient historical accident has set us off down one particular path, only one way is remotely available; it has become a "virtual necessity" ' (Dennett 1995: 129). In short, there is an absolute requirement in biological evolution for species-specific description; there is a level at which, taking Gould rather out of context, the only option is to 'celebrate diversity and revel in the peculiarities of animals' (Gould 1991: 171). We need to sift through what history has left behind to understand the fact that some rhinos have one horn but others have two; or the fact that the elephant and rhino are similar in general physical characteristics and in habitat, but only one has evolved a trunk from an ancestral nose; or the fact that the dominant mammals in the Old World are placental, but those in Australia are marsupial. It would be possible, but essentially pointless, to propose violable constraints requiring four-leggedness, or marsupialness, or a constraint against trunks which is incredibly high-ranking except in elephants; what we really need is just a recognition that there are some facts we can perfectly adequately describe, but not explain except in terms of historical contingency.

Opinion is divided over the extent to which Gould and Lewontin's arguments challenge mainstream neo-Darwinist thinking: as Pinker and Bloom (1990: 709) aptly summarize, 'The Gould and Lewontin argument could be interpreted as stressing that because the neo-Darwinian theory of evolution includes nonadaptationist processes, it is bad scientific practice not to test them as alternatives to natural selection in any particular instance. However, they are often read as having outlined a radical new alternative to Darwin, in which natural selection is relegated to a minor role.' Pinker and Bloom themselves favour the first view, and we shall adduce further evidence for it in Chapter 5 below, in a consideration of the role of natural selection in the evolution of language. Certainly, although Gould and Lewontin have shown that adaptation and natural selection are not sufficient to account for all biological traits, these mechanisms still seem necessary. Dennett (1995) defends adaptationism as a lynchpin of evolutionary theory, criticizing Gould and Lewontin for attacking an extreme view which no-one actually holds, and accepting that not all traits can appropriately be seen as adaptive. As Cronin (1991: 86) puts it, ' ... natural selection could be the only true begetter of adaptations without having begot all characteristics; one can hold that all adaptive characteristics are the result of natural selection without holding that all characteristics are, indeed, adaptive.'

Nonetheless, although Gould and Lewontin may to some extent be criticizing a panadaptationist caricature, they raise the serious question of how adaptationist explanations can ever be ruled out, if general plausibility is the only criterion for accepting them. It may be that 'plausible stories can always be told. The key to historical research lies in devising criteria to identify proper explanations among the substantial set of plausible pathways to any modern result' (Gould and Lewontin 1979: 588). In biological terms, this means we first require a set of constraints, some of which will be universal and derivable from the laws of physics or from deep functional trends underlying and unifying disparate biological processes. Some properties of organisms will arise, directly and transparently, from the inviolable constraints. Others will reflect a suspension of a defeasible constraint, often for adaptive reasons arising from the environment of the organism concerned. Finally, there is variation between species, each having its own unique properties. Although these answer to the constraints, which delimit the space for possible variation, they are also influenced by the starting state for any particular evolutionary development and, again, the environment. Each species will require a degree of independent description in isolation from the constraints, since it represents the current stage in a long chain of changes, some of which refine the results of originally random events. Prediction is impossible at this level, although if we take a detailed enough historical perspective, we may understand where the differences between groups have come from. These descriptive statements, the biological analogue of phonological rules, will then reflect the interaction of chance, the species and the environment within a framework created by the constraints.

Evolutionary biology then faces various challenges. Most importantly, a rationale must be developed for distinguishing these three levels of absolute universal laws, violable constraints and species-specific description. The mere appearance of adaptiveness is not enough: 'when a flying fish leaves the water, it is extremely adaptive for it to reenter the water. But we do not need natural selection to explain this happy event; gravity will do just fine' (Pinker 1994: 358). It might be attractive to propose a first-order division according to what the superordinate principles, like the scaling laws and absolute physical constraints like gravity, cannot account for. This, however, is only going to work if we have some way of preventing the formulation of new 'laws' (such as a putative Law of Eye Formation to account for the recurrent evolution of the eye in different species (Pinker and Bloom 1990); we shall see in Chapter 5 that such steps are unnecessary). Furthermore, it is important that we should at least attempt to understand what underlies the universal laws; hence the importance of West, Brown and Enquist (1997) in relating the scaling laws to fractals.

A further line will then have to be drawn between what can be explained using adaptive reasoning and what cannot. Sober (1990: 764) argues that ' "Why do rhinoceri have horns?" is a very different question from, "Why do rhinoceri have precisely the number of horns they do?" ', with only the former explicable in adaptive terms, perhaps with reference to self-defence. If one rhino species has one horn and another two, this will instead result from 'purely historical factors concerning the state of the two ancestral populations.' Unfortunately, although the difference between the two explananda may be clear with hindsight, the questions themselves are deceptively similar. In fact, it is arguably impossible to isolate a class of facts which adaption could not conceivably account for, at least *a priori*: as we have seen, plausible adaptive stories can potentially be told anywhere. To take an example, human groups vary in tooth shape. No pattern seems particularly beneficial or detrimental; we simply have variation, which has arisen historically for whatever reason, and being genetically controlled, is now propagated through populations. There is nothing to stop us proposing a constraint against any particular tooth shape, such as tooth shovelling, which can be violated in certain circumstances, but this is no more enlightening than simply describing the situation, and perhaps seeking a historical account of the origin of the phenomenon (which might tell us other interesting things, like which human groups are more closely related). Gould and Lewontin (1979) do suggest experimental methods of testing proposed adaptive explanations, and associated constraints; but they also note that, before even contemplating the necessity of carrying out such tests, theorists will have to overcome their tendency to force all biological phenomena into the same category. The intuitive appeal of a Theory of Everything is very strong.

We return, then, to Optimality Theory, where phonologists face a precisely parallel problem. The prospect of interacting constraints and nothing but interacting constraints as the conditioning factor for all phonological phenomena is extremely appealing. However, as we saw in Chapters 2 and 3, this will not work. Evidence from other models inside and outside linguistics shows that this conclusion should not surprise us: universal laws, universal tendencies and system-specific descriptions are all perfectly normal and expected ingredients of theories as divergent as Natural Morphology and evolutionary biology. And in both those cases, we face an additional difficulty, which OT must also confront, of distinguishing between these classes of statements. This problem is most acute at the lowest level, in separating phenomena ascribable to universal but defeasible constraints from those only describable by system-specific rules. This distinction will remain problematic so long as phonologists persist in proposing ever-increasing numbers of constraints, which purport to be universal, but in fact encode purely language-specific information.

In fact, phonology already enjoys a possible advantage over the other systems we have reviewed, in incorporating two actual formal mechanisms, constraints and rules, which are suited to universal and system-specific statements respectively. This may also reflect the fact that phonology has two poles, one more cognitive and the other closer to the surface phonetic level, perhaps another indication that we might not be dealing with a single class of phenomena. As we have seen, there may be further divisions, with prosodic phonology apparently more amenable to description in terms of constraints. If this observation turns out to be robust, one focus for future research would involve looking for reasons why prosodic phenomena seem more responsive to universal constraints.

Prince and Smolensky (1993: 14) complain of 'the formal arbitrariness characteristic of re-writing rules when they are put to the task of dealing locally with problems that fall under general principles.' In the light of our discussion so far, it seems doubtful whether all phonological phenomena do fall under such principles: descriptive tools are therefore also required, and OT faces the task of distinguishing between system-specific descriptors and universal, if violable, constraints. However, regardless of the outcome of this ongoing research, it is unlikely to remove, or even significantly diminish, the reliance of OT on innate constraints and mechanisms. In that case, it seems reasonable to ask how these innate components may have arisen in the human species. In the next chapter, then, we return to biological evolution, this time not as a metaphor, nor even as a cognate discipline which has confronted certain common problems in a way which might be illuminating for linguistics, but to consider current thinking on the evolution of language, and its implications for OT.

5

The Emergence of the Innate: Evolving Optimality

5.1 The nature of innateness

In the orthodox Optimality Theory view, phonological Universal Grammar consists of the function Gen, plus a list of innate, universal and violable constraints. The question to be explored in this chapter is whether a richly structured Universal Grammar of this kind could reasonably have evolved in our species by the mechanisms usually thought to be responsible for the development of complex systems. If the alleged development of such a system cannot be reconciled with the normal forces of evolution, then good arguments will have to be provided for seeing it as the product of some other, special processes. If no convincing arguments are available, we have a further, more general reason for seeing this picture of phonology as inadequate.

The justification of innateness in evolutionary terms has not been much of an issue in linguistics up to now, probably for two main reasons. First, we shall see below that Chomsky quite clearly sees the evolution of language as out of the ordinary, and beyond the scope of the neo-Darwinian model considered in the last chapter. Secondly, there has been a lengthy period, since the topic of the origin of language was banned by the Linguistic Society of Paris in 1866, during which the evolution of language has not been part of mainstream linguistics. This area has, however, been very considerably rehabilitated over the last decade, as evidenced by seminal papers like Pinker and Bloom (1990); a number of recent books, including Kirby (1999) and Carstairs-McCarthy

(1999); and a series of dedicated international conferences beginning in 1996, which do not involve only, or even primarily, linguists, but reflect a growing trend towards interdisciplinary work featuring anthropologists, neurobiologists, primatologists, computer scientists and others (Hurford, Studdert-Kennedy and Knight 1998). It is now clear that we can and should consider strongly innatist theories like OT in the light of this emerging synthesis on the evolution of language: 'Linguistics, as the study of human language, cannot be complete without a component on its origins' (Hurford 1992: 300).

Before proceeding to a more detailed discussion of the origins of language, however, two clarifications are necessary: these are partly terminological, and partly deeper issues. First, 'linguistic evolution' is a deeply ambiguous phrase, and refers both to language change of the attested or reconstructed type, say from one word order type to another, and to the development of the human capacity for language in our species, if not *ex nihilo*, then at least ex something else (see below). There has been a good deal of recent discussion on the electronic Histling list generally discouraging the use of 'evolution' for the former, and it does indeed seem reasonable to distinguish the human tendency to acquire and use language on the one hand, from the phenotypic developments of languages as products within the bounds defined by that species-specific capacity on the other. Hurford (1992) uses the terms glossogenetic evolution for ongoing change, and phylogenetic evolution for the initial development of the human language faculty. It is true that, for an evolutionary biologist, evolution is recognized as an ongoing process; but it is also an extremely slow one, and in language, we are dealing with a very recently developed phenomenon in a very recently developed species, with a long generation interval to boot. It is therefore at least a fair bet that nothing much will have changed at the genetic level during the relatively brief period in which humans have 'had' language in something like its current form, justifying what might seem a rather artificial distinction between language change and true evolution.

The second issue is just what we mean by 'at the genetic level'. In fact, there are two levels underlying observable linguistic behaviour. Linguists find it convenient and enlightening to analyse linguistic output, performance or E-language, in terms of more abstract but still linguistic components of competence or I-language: these might be phonological rules, OT constraints, or Chomskyan Principles and Parameters. At this second level, some of the formal objects we postulate are descriptive tools formulated by the linguist to expose generalizations of which the language user is tacitly aware: this would be true of rules. Others, however, are claimed to be innate, and therefore inherited: constraints, principles and parameters would fall into this category. These innate structures, under a very usual assumption of autonomy (Newmeyer 1991), will be seen as restricted to language, but do not determine linguistic behaviour directly; rather, they are mediated by the linguistic data the language learner hears, which shapes them in particular ways, for instance allowing the ranking of the innate OT constraints, or setting the parameters of Chomskyan syntax.

Underlying these mental structures, however, there must be a third and final genetic stage. The OT constraints requiring nuclei or preferring onsets, like the Subjacency Condition or the parameter specifying VO or OV word order, and like any other mental or physical organ giving rise to particular effects or behaviour in the world, cannot be directly genetically encoded. Instead, there must be a level of genetic instructions, which in the case of language presumably direct the development of hard-wired circuits in the brain, allowing or favouring the learning of language systems which conform to particular criteria. In discussing the evolution of language in our species, then, we are considering the development of genetic instructions to create (or recruit) mental circuits, forming what we might call a language organ or language acquisition device; this is open to further structuring under the influence of external linguistic data, and eventually gives rise to an internal grammar, itself allowing production and perception of concrete linguistic behaviour. The genes underlying language are currently extremely imperfectly understood, and their contribution is only beginning to be inferred from their role in familial linguistic pathologies: for instance, a particular genetic marker on chromosome 7 has been found to co-occur with cases of specific language impairment (Ridley 1999). It is therefore natural that we should focus, in a discussion of the evolution of language, on the second, intermediate level of formal statements governing the possibility and frequency of linguistic structures, such as the OT constraints. In doing so, however, we must bear in mind that we are already abstracting away from a deeper, genetic level.

5.2   Language, complexity, and design

5.2.1   *Central questions*

Pinker (1994: 332–3) observes, uncontroversially, that although the elephant's trunk is a development of original nose and upper lip muscles, the resulting trunk is unique to elephants. He then speculates that, if biologists were elephants, they would become obsessed with this unique organ, and would fall into two classes in their attempts to deal with its implications. The first group would attempt to find some precursor to the trunk, or at least some similar properties, in the hyrax, which is the closest living relative of the elephant. On the other hand,

The opposite school, maintaining the uniqueness of the trunk, might insist that it appeared all at once in the offspring of a particular trunk-less elephant ancestor, the product of a single dramatic mutation. Or they might say that the trunk somehow arose as an automatic by-product of the elephant's having evolved a large head. They might add another paradox for trunk evolution: the trunk is absurdly more intricate and well coordinated than any ancestral elephant would have needed.

Precisely parallel arguments for language, as a property apparently unique to humans, are to be encountered in the literature. Language is sometimes seen as an obstacle to Darwinian evolution, either because there are no generally accepted precursors or congeners in other apes, or because the system is apparently so complex that natural selection cannot have succeeded in developing it. There is also a further objection to language as a product of natural selection: we saw in Chapter 4 that traits which spread through selection are very frequently advantageous to an individual, but some aspects of language are seen as maladaptive, jeopardizing the analysis of language as a product of the normal mechanisms of evolution. In the following two sections, we shall address these issues in more detail: 5.2.2 assesses the arguments around gradualism, while 5.2.3 focuses on the adaptive nature of human language.

5.2.2 *Gradualism and the evolution of language*

Dawkins (1986: 1) defines biology as 'the study of complicated things that give the appearance of having been designed for a purpose'; moreover, in his terms, 'a complex thing is something whose constituent parts are arranged in a way that is unlikely to have arisen by chance alone' (1986: 7). The theory of evolution provides an account of how small and simple changes, each of which could plausibly have arisen by chance, can by a long process of gradual accumulation produce a coordinated and streamlined system adapted to a particular task. Indeed, and recall here Dennett's (1995: 68) Principle of the Accumulation of Design, it may appear to have been created for that very purpose. Although we need not assume direct creation, we do require the hypothesis that the function or behaviour which this novel system allows is of some benefit (or was, at the time it developed), entailing its propagation by natural selection.

Human language would appear to meet these criteria. It is undeniably a complex system even in its phenotypic manifestations; it involves structures in the brain, ear and vocal organs; it is composed in itself of numerous interacting levels and structures; and it is good for something, which we might define simplistically, leaving further discussion in abeyance until the next section, as communication. In these respects it is similar, as Pinker and

Bloom (1990) argue, to other complex abilities like echolocation in bats, and might be expected to be amenable to explanation in the same kind of way, involving partially adaptive reasoning, and the mechanism of natural selection, the prime mover in the evolution of complex systems.

If we consider the eye, to take the example of a well-understood but complex structure, a neo-Darwinian explanation would begin with a mutation enabling some cell to detect light, which one might regard as an extremely rudimentary form of vision: since this would confer advantages in terms of survival and reproduction, it would become frequent in the population; and it would also be built upon very gradually, eventually producing a structure conferring considerable visual acuity. One might initially challenge this gradualist view by questioning the time which such complex systems would take to evolve: for the eye, this argument has been neutralized by Nilsson and Pelger (1994), who note that Darwin himself believed the eye might constitute a problem for his theory of natural selection. Nilsson and Pelger designed computer simulations of the evolution of an eye, beginning with 'a patch of pigmented light-sensitive epithelium' and modelling successive 1 per cent modifications of this existing tissue, each increasing marginally the spatial information the primitive eye could detect. Even though Nilsson and Pelger introduced a number of conservative and pessimistic elements into their calculations, such as the assumption that each new generation could only differ in respect of one part of the eye, whereas in reality changes would be much more likely to occur in parallel, their model took only 1829 1 per cent steps to 'evolve' a camera-type eye, complete with lens, of the sort found in fish and cephalopods. On the conservative estimate that only a 0.005 per cent change, rather than a whole 1 per cent, would take place in a generation, Nilsson and Pelger arrive at a figure of 363,992 generations for the eye to evolve from a piece of flat skin by natural selection. If each generation takes a year, as is the case for many small aquatic animals, this gives a time period of less than 364,000 years: given that fossils with evidence of eyes are attested from approximately 550 million years Before Present, 'the time passed since then is enough for eyes to evolve more than 1500 times!' (Nilsson and Pelger 1994). Small wonder, as Dawkins (1995: 96–7) observes, that ' "the" eye has evolved at least forty times independently around the animal kingdom'. Returning to language, Pinker (1994) similarly points out that the common ancestor of humans and chimps lived around 5–7 million years ago, a period of approximately 350,000 generations which allows ample time for the evolution of even complex systems. The apparent uniqueness of human language is also not an obstacle here: intermediates might have existed, but have died out, and since chimps are then only the species closest to humans because of 'the accidents of extinction' (Pinker 1994: 346), whether they did or did not have some precursor of language is of no particular relevance.

Even if we accept this, we face a further argument, which following Dawkins (1995: 81) we may call 'the Argument from Personal Incredulity': this essentially questions the development of a highly structured system from many intermediate stages. Its proponents query the selective advantage intermediate stages might confer, as we shall see in the next section, and tend to prefer a one-step, macromutational origin for a complex system, rather than a gradualist approach. In linguistic terms, we might adduce here Bickerton's view, paraphrased by Pinker (1997: 202), that 'a single mutation in a single woman, African Eve, simultaneously wired in syntax, resized and reshaped the skull and reworked the vocal tract'. Similarly, Chomsky's work reflects his view that language is unique and therefore beyond the reach of conventional evolutionary theory, which, as he sees it, 'appears to have very little to say … about any kind of innovation. It can explain how you get a different distribution of qualities that are already present, but does not say much about how new qualities can emerge' (1982: 23). Properties of UG are then 'simply emergent properties of a brain that reaches a certain level of complexity under the specific conditions of human evolution' (Chomsky 1991: 50), and language is the result of physical principles and mechanisms we currently do not understand: 'We know very little about what happens when 10^{10} neurons are crammed into something the size of a basketball' (Chomsky 1975: 59). This reduces the origin of language to 'what is, essentially, a "packing problem"' (Newmeyer 1998a: 314).

However, the Argument from Personal Incredulity also fails to stand up to close scrutiny, for two reasons. First, gradual accumulations of complexity are much more likely to lead to a favourable outcome than a single great leap, however tempting the latter is intuitively. As Dawkins (1986: 73) puts it,

because ... the number of different ways of being dead is so much greater than the number of different ways of being alive, the chances are very high that a big random jump in genetic space will end in death. Even a small random jump in genetic space is pretty likely to end in death. But the smaller the jump the less likely death is, and the more likely is it that the jump will result in improvement.

The calculations underlying this assumption are to be found in Fisher (1930); more accessibly and memorably, Pinker (1994: 362) compares the likelihood of a single-jump, or saltationist origin for a complex organ or system to the possibility of a hurricane in a junkyard spontaneously assembling a fully functioning Boeing 747. In other words (Pinker 1997: 198),

It is not that large mutations and rapid change violate some law of evolution. It is only that complex engineering requires precise arrangements of delicate parts, and if the engineering is accomplished by accumulating random changes, those changes had better be small. Complex organs evolve by small steps for the same reason that a watchmaker does not use a sledgehammer and a surgeon does not use a meat cleaver.

Secondly, Chomsky relies on the assumption that Universal Grammar arose *de novo*; and yet the parts of the human brain involved in language perception and production are not without homologues in related species: homologues of Broca's area in monkey brains are involved in control of the muscles of the face, mouth, tongue and larynx, and also in receiving sensory input from hearing and touch, while homologues of Wernicke's area are important in recognizing sound sequences and discriminating one's own calls from those of other monkeys (Deacon 1997): these arguably 'gave evolution some parts it could tinker with to produce the human language circuitry' (Pinker 1997: 191). Furthermore, since normal language can be found in some people with unusually small brains, and conversely specific language impairment is observed in speakers with brains of normal shape and size, 'All the evidence suggests that it is the precise wiring of the brain's microcircuitry that makes language happen, not gross size, shape, or neuron packing' (Pinker 1997: 200).

However, this gradualist scenario does require intermediate stages, which are not directly attested, although admittedly it is not difficult to imagine them: we need only think of the two-word stage in children acquiring a first language; or the structures of pidgins; or the rudimentary strings achieved by chimps taught to use signs. One might assume that more direct evidence for such steps might come from computer simulations: recall Nilsson and Pelger's successful modelling of the development of the eye. However, although there has been considerable recent activity in this area (Kirby 1998, 1999; Batali 1998; Nettle 1999*a,b,c*; Briscoe forthcoming), 'The organisms involved are very simple and not particularly realistic. They typically have very few possible behaviours and a simplified spatial world' (Nettle 1999*a*: 38). Furthermore, so many initial conditions have to be built into most of these simulations, with a good deal of structure being supplied to begin with, that they are essentially modelling language change rather than language origins. In short, they tell us a good deal that is interesting and relevant about the development of relatively complex structures from relatively simple ones, but they also recall the saying that the programmer's control over the initial conditions means simulations are doomed to success.

Simulations are, however, increasingly recognizing the important role of social factors in both language change and linguistic evolution. Notably, Nettle (1999*a*) finds that group size is vital in deriving significant inter-group differences in phoneme learning, and that social selection, with learners preferentially copying

high-status individuals, also significantly amplifies developing diversity. This work reflects a trend in work on language
evolution to emphasize the contribution of the sociocultural context, as seen, for instance, in Dunbar's (1996, 1998) hypothesis that
language developed as a less time-consuming replacement for
grooming, and functioned to keep social groups together, or
Power's (1998) suggestion that female kin-bonding and menstrual
coalitions were particularly important in establishing the reliability of vocal signals among subordinate females, who faced particular problems in balancing their time–energy budgets. Although
these social factors need not be discussed in detail here, they do
shade into the next issue: if we assume that gradual steps could in
principle lead to the development of a complex system, we have
to establish that natural selection would have motivated this accumulation of gradual steps, which is more likely if the intermediate stages confer some advantage.

5.2.3   Selective advantage and the evolution
    of language

Returning to the eye, Dawkins (1995: 89) argues that although good
vision is needed for reading, someone with poorer eyesight could
still play tennis; very limited visual acuity will give enough warning
to stop someone falling off a cliff; and even less will still allow dis-
crimination of night from day. That is, 'there is a continuum of
tasks to which an eye might be put, such that for any given quality of eye, from magnificent to terrible, there is a level of task at
which a marginal improvement in vision would make all the difference.' Dawkins (1986: 81) similarly suggests that 'in a primitive
world where some creatures had no eyes at all and others had
lensless eyes, the ones with lensless eyes would have all sorts of
advantages.' Even in a world and in a species where relatively good
vision is the norm, an individual is likely to prefer limited vision
to none at all: if you lose your glasses, you don't go around with
your eyes shut until you find them again (Dawkins 1986: 81).

Moreover, this defence against the Argument from Personal Incredulity extends to other systems (Dawkins 1986: 91):

Whenever we have an X in a real live animal, where X is some organ too complex to have arisen by chance in a single step, then according to the theory of evolution by natural selection it must be the case that a fraction of an X is better than no X at all; and two fractions of an X must be better than one; and a whole X must be better than nine-tenths of an X.

In terms of behavioural systems which are perhaps more closely comparable with language, many species mimic others, but the mimicry need not be perfect to be useful at some level. Biologists can check the reactions of organisms by using mimicry too. For instance, male sticklebacks have red bellies, and if they are confronted with even a very crude dummy stickleback with a red patch in approximately the right place, they will threaten it; Dawkins (1995: 84) here relates that a red mail van passed Niko Tinbergen's laboratory one day, provoking all his male stickle-backs to rush to the window side of their tank and threaten that. In situations where prey species fool predators by mimicking bark or leaves, natural selection might be responsible for improving the mimicry so that it is effective at a shorter distance, or in broad daylight rather than just at dusk. If we find a caterpillar which appears to mimic a piece of bark perfectly, we can assume that intermediate stages existed whereby the mimicry was rather less convincing, with death at the beaks of predatory birds enforcing selection of the more bark-like results. Similarly, if we consider bee dancing, we can hypothesize earlier stages with less complex choreography: for example (Dawkins 1995: 102ff), Von Frisch found more limited versions of the honeybee dance in its modern relatives, notably *Apis florea*, the dwarf bee, and argued on this basis that the dance initially constituted ritually repeated versions of the take-off run executed by a bee about to return for more pollen. Natural selection would favour a prolonged or exaggerated run if this encouraged more bees to follow. Nonetheless,

Dawkins (1995: 102) points out that it is misleading to see these earlier dances as incomplete:

No creature makes a living at being an 'incomplete', 'intermediate stage'. The ancient, long-dead bees whose dances can be interpreted, with hindsight, as intermediates on the way to the modern honeybee dance made a good living. They lived full bee lives and had no thought of being 'on the way' to something 'better'. Moreover, our 'modern' bee dance may not be the last word but may evolve into something even more spectacular when we and our bees are gone.

Although human language might on the face of it seem to share enough features with these other evolved systems to strongly support a hypothesis of gradual evolution by natural selection, not all linguists have taken this view. On the contrary, Chomsky (1988: 167) contends that 'It surely cannot be assumed that every trait is specifically selected. In the case of such systems as language or wings it is not even easy to imagine a course of selection that might have given rise to them. A rudimentary wing, for example, is not "useful" for motion but is more of an impediment.' As we saw in the last section, Chomsky prefers to ascribe the evolution of language to 'reasons that have to do with the biology of cells, to be explained in terms of properties of physical mechanisms, now unknown', or to 'the operation of physical laws applying to a brain of a certain degree of complexity' (1988: 169–70). Similarly, Piattelli-Palmarini (1989) rejects an adaptationist and selectionist view of language origins in favour of a model giving greater weight to larger-scale genetic transformations involving transposable elements or 'jumping genes', which can have major developmental effects, or hitch-hiking genes which attach themselves to other genes with effects which may be selected. According to Piattelli-Palmarini (1989: 8), 'what the new evolutionary theory is saying is that full-blown evolutionary novelty can also suddenly arise, so to speak, *for no reason*, because novelty caused by sheer proximity between genes is not governed by function and it, therefore, eludes strict adaptationism.' We therefore see a move, led by linguists, towards seeing language as either an output of non-selectionist genetic mechanisms, or as a spandrel (see Chapter 4 above) arising from physical laws triggered, for instance, by an increase in hominid brain size. Either way, language ceases to be a product of gradualist evolution, and becomes an emergent property, a system which arose all at once: in genetics, such major single innovations are known as hopeful monsters.

In view of Gould and Lewontin's (1979) views, surveyed in Chapter 4 above, on the unwarranted dominance of adaptationist argumentation in evolutionary theory, it is perhaps unsurprising to find Gould agreeing with Chomsky that language may be an automatic by-product of brain capacity: however, Dennett (1995: 391) argues that 'these two authorities are supporting each other over an abyss.' Gould and Lewontin were quite right to point out that natural selection cannot *a priori* be accepted as the only mechanism involved in evolution, even in any particular case, and that alternative mechanisms should be considered and tested; but even work establishing these alternatives mechanisms, in the form of transposons, hitch-hiking and so on, has accepted that their overall role in evolution is likely to be extremely minor. Large-scale changes also characteristically modify or duplicate existing structures; for instance, a transposable element-induced mutation could lead to fruit flies having legs where their antennae should be, but biologists would normally rule out a single, major genetic change as the cause of legs or antennae arising *de novo* in a species: recall Dawkins's assertion that most large genetic leaps would axiomatically end in death or in monsters which are pretty much hopeless, and highly unlikely to bequeath their monstrous tendencies to future generations. Furthermore, as Pinker and Bloom (1990: 712) argue, 'there are clear criteria for when selectionist and nonselectionist accounts should be invoked to explain some biological structure: complex design to carry out some reproductively significant function, versus the existence of a specific physical developmental, or random process capable of explaining the structure's existence.' And it is not enough to invoke physical laws as yet unidentified, an approach which Pinker and Bloom (1990: 711) characterize as 'empty and non-falsifiable.'

'Of course', they continue, 'human brains *obey* the laws of physics, and always did, but that does not mean that their specific structure can be *explained* by such laws' (1990: 720). As we saw in Chapter 4, general laws can provide a framework, but there is a species-specific level beyond this where the accidents of history interact with general mechanisms to produce unpredictable results: as Deacon (1997: 46) tells us, 'Evolution is the epitome of inscrutability and opportunism—seldom following an obvious or elegant path.' Invoking mutation and natural selection provide well-understood routes for the development of complexity and apparent design under such circumstances.

Linguists opposing a selectionist view of the evolution of language also rely on a variant of the Argument from Personal Incredulity, suggesting that particular aspects of UG cannot possibly be advantageous to an organism. Perhaps the most succinct statement of this type is Lightfoot's (1991*b*: 68–9) contention that 'the Subjacency Condition has many virtues, but I am not sure that it could have increased the chances of having fruitful sex.' An answer to this point must address two issues: first, whether or not individual aspects of UG could have any beneficial impact of any kind, for instance in terms of improving the chances of successful communication; and second, whether this in turn might be expected to increase one's chances of successful reproduction.

There do seem to be recurrent doubts about the usefulness of elements of UG. Premack (1985: 281–2), in a more detailed development of Lightfoot's point but for a different principle, lays down the gauntlet:

I challenge the reader to reconstruct the scenario that would confer selective fitness on recursiveness ... Would it be a great advantage for one of our ancestors squatting alongside the embers, to be able to remark: 'Beware of the short beast whose front hoof Bob cracked when, having forgotten his own spear back at camp, he got in a glancing blow with the dull spear he borrowed from Jack'?

Premack's argument reduces to two points we have already encountered: first, natural selection can only play a part in the evolution of a trait which is positively and actively beneficial; and second, certain linguistic structures, like the elephant's trunk, are far too powerful for the job they have to do, and certainly for the job they presumably had to do at their inception, so that consequently, trunks, like language, must have evolved by a single giant mutation rather than gradually. Indeed, Lightfoot explicitly expresses a preference for a view of Subjacency as 'one component of a large-scale mutation, involving a package of new properties' (1991*b*: 69). We are back in hopeful monster territory here.

To return to function, Newmeyer (1991: 15) holds that Subjacency does indeed 'ease communicators' burdens', thus increasing the efficiency of communication, and argues that 'surely, an advance in the ability to convey complex propositions clearly and unambiguously should have done as much for the survival of early hominids as, say, minute variations in the shape of a finch's beak or the color of a squirrel's coat have aided the survival of such creatures.' Pinker (1994: 367) provides a parallel rationale for recursiveness, noting its involvement in many constructions much simpler than Premack's example, including *I think he left*, and *the man's hat*, while Pinker and Bloom (1990: 723) see recursion as advantageous in conveying information: 'For example, it makes a big difference whether a far-off region … has animals that you can eat or animals that can eat you.' In general, biologists find no difficulty with this line of argumentation: as Ridley (1999: 105) observes,

It is easy to conceive how it was advantageous for our ancestors on the plains of Africa to share detailed and precise information with each other at a level of sophistication unavailable to other species. 'Go a short way up that valley and turn left by the tree in front of the pond and you will find the giraffe carcass we just killed. Avoid the brush on the right of the tree that is in fruit, because we saw a lion go in there.' Two sentences pregnant with survival value to the recipient; two tickets for success in the natural-selection lottery, yet wholly incomprehensible without a capacity for understanding grammar, and lots of it.

A language manifesting Subjacency and recursion would then improve the chances of successful communication; genetic instructions to configure the brain in such a way as to learn such a system would be preferentially inherited. On this view, language evolved as a mosaic, with individual parts of UG being introduced gradually, new circuitry being built, and other structures recruited and redeployed; and we can adapt Dawkins's (1995: 90) view of the utility of the eye to language: 'Half an eye is just 1 per-cent better than 49 percent of an eye, which is already better than 48 percent, and the difference is significant.' Furthermore, the whole system may be beneficial without this being true of every component: to assume that every element must be adaptive and selected for individually is 'hyper-selectionism', which Darwin himself rejected (Newmeyer 1998a: 309). We must remember that evolution works with whatever initial structures come to hand: in this light, it is unsurprising that UG is 'an evolutionary comprom-ise, nonoptimal from the point of view of any subtask that it has to perform, but nevertheless shaped by selection to carry out the ensemble of tasks as well as evolution could "arrange" for it to do' (Newmeyer 1998a: 310).

Lightfoot, however, does not only want to know that Sub-jacency has a plausible rationale in resolving parsing problems, for instance: in addition, 'one wants to know why this solution was adopted' (1991b: 68). We can assume that the answer depends in part on historical contextual influences outside our knowl-edge: thus, just as we can give an adaptive reason for the rhino's horn(s), but not for the number of horns an individual species has, we can argue for a benefit in improving parsing, but not predict which strategy might be adopted to permit this. In fact, Newmeyer (1991) does go some way to answering Lightfoot's question with his speculation that the principles he considers, including Subjacency, are functionally asymmetric: that is, they favour the hearer at the expense of making communicational life more difficult for the speaker. Newmeyer argues that principles of this sort will have to become biologized to be perpetuated: it is unnecessary to impute factors facilitating communication for both speaker and hearer to UG, as both would converge on them inevitably in any case. It might also be noted that Lightfoot's stance in this instance has changed over time. Romaine (1981: 284), in a review of Lightfoot (1979), argues that his proposed Transparency Principle is inadequate, since 'to "explain" syntactic change to the fullest extent, we would have to predict both the change and its mechanism', something the Transparency Principle avowedly cannot do. Lightfoot (1981: 363), in response, observes drily: 'I think that she is too ambitious. Her theory will need to be able to predict at least which stylistic innovations speakers will make and when, and what and when they will borrow from a neighbouring language ... perhaps she will achieve such a theory in future work; meanwhile I am not holding my breath.'

In short, then, the important thing is to understand the general mechanisms and their applicability. There are problems which must be surmounted to improve vision, or linguistic communication (if you happen to be a human), or echolocation (if you happen to be a bat), but the contingencies of history determine the solution selected, and these may be irrecoverable, as may the intermediate structures which led to the present-day situation. Presumably the lack of fossil precursors to the wing accounts for Chomsky's use of this system as an analogy for language: recall his view that 'In the case of such systems as language or wings it is not even easy to imagine a course of selection that might have given rise to them. A rudimentary wing, for example, is not "useful" for motion but is more of an impediment' (1988: 167). Morell (1997), however, reports the discovery of a 90-million-year-old fossil dinosaur in Argentina, which appears to have folded up its forelimbs as if they were wings. This creature, named *Unenlagia com-ahuensis* 'half-bird from northwest Patagonia', could also have stretched its wing-like arms out for balance, in a manner reminiscent of birds about to take flight. Its arm and shoulder anatomy may indicate the changes necessary for a transition from dinosaurs to birds. Although our theoretical stance predicts an equivalent earlier existence of intermediate forms of language, the lack of linguistic fossils means evidence of these is highly unlikely to be forthcoming. However, we may simply have to reconcile ourselves to this as a corollary of studying a 'soft' and unpreservable system: 'we may never be able to confirm the details, but if so this will not be a mystery but only a bit of irreparable ignorance' (Dennett 1995: 389).

We return, courtesy of Lightfoot (1991*b*), to the putative connection of Subjacency with reproductive success. Given that Subjacency, and other aspects of UG, are envisaged as part of a system dedicated to language, it is indeed impossible that they should make reproduction more likely by any direct means, exerting some benign influence, for instance, on sperm motility or egg quality. Language, however, also has an observable behavioural aspect, and all sorts of ostensibly unlikely observable traits can in fact improve the chances of an organism leaving descendants. The peacock's tail is undoubtedly a dreadful encumbrance in many ways, and I have not seen a directly adaptive account of its utility during mating (say, by improving balance). On the other hand, peahens appear to favour peacocks with large tails, inferring that these specimens are genetically so well equipped that they can afford to divert precious energy away from the ordinary everyday requirements of living, towards the growth and upkeep of this extraneous, if attractive, organ. Linguistic proficiency might also help in attracting, or keeping, a mate. Indeed, 'anthropologists have noted that tribal chiefs are often both gifted orators and highly polygynous—a splendid prod to any imagination that cannot conceive of how linguistic skills could make a Darwinian difference' (Pinker 1994: 369). In short, Lightfoot is certainly right in assuming that Subjacency and its like do not directly improve the organism's chances of having fruitful sex; but if better language increases your chances of having sex at all, and improves your choice of partner, then that is highly likely to contribute to your chances of reproducing if everything else is in working order.

5.3 Evolving Optimality

Although we have concentrated so far on UG as envisaged in Chomskyan principles and parameters theory, OT is strikingly similar in many respects. Since the constraints of OT, as well as

Gen, are taken to be innate, we must therefore make a case for their evolution as part of the mosaic that underlies language. In fact, there are two problems for OT in evolutionary terms; the particular problem which is relevant depends on whether the constraint system is regarded as fixed or flexible. In short, if the innate constraints form an indivisible set, then language must have evolved by some single macromutation; but if novel constraints can develop, and become innate, then OT may be a Lamarckian system.

From the discussion above, it would appear that the only tenable view of the evolution of complex and apparently designed systems involves the gradual operation of natural selection. As we have seen, however, Chomsky refutes this view of the evolution of language, preferring to see UG as having developed *de novo* in a single step (although he does leave room for the possible refinement of the language capacity by the subsequent action of natural selection (1988: 167)). It would appear that UG then constitutes a closed system, with no alteration or addition possible; as Piattelli-Palmarini (1989: 20–1) defines it, anything the 'envelope' of innate possibilities allows is legitimate, but anything it rules out is prohibited. Individual and group variation arise solely from the interaction of this fixed innate component with the primary linguistic data, but the 'envelope' formed by the innate component cannot admit anything new. Evolution by natural selection involves variation at the phenotypic level, based on variation at the genetic level, since mutation will occur here, and will create variants which are heritable. The genes that build eyes are therefore different from person to person (let alone from species to species), although admittedly natural selection will tend to minimize this variation in the sense that any mutation causing gross dysfunction or complete lack of function, whether involving a single gene of large effect or multiple genes with cumulative small effects, will not typically be passed on by reproduction. If we then accept that gene frequencies under mutation can vary randomly, the chance of their producing consistently an identical product, in the shape of the fixed contents of UG, is vanishingly small. If the constraints of Optimality Theory are similarly all innate and universal, and form a closed set, there can be no room in the system for future evolution of this kind. Since there is no evidence of evolution stopping in evolved systems, it also follows that such a closed set cannot *have* evolved by mutation and natural selection. The only option is then to assume saltation, or to derive the constraints wholesale as an emergent property following from brain size, for instance: but as we have seen, these hypotheses involve mechanisms marginal to evolutionary biology, and certainly not suited to complex adaptive systems in the way that natural selection arguably is. In adopting this approach we would certainly, in Pinker's (1994: 369) words, be trying 'to portray language as innate, complex and useful but not a product of the one force in nature that can make innate complex useful things.'

It might then be tempting to circumvent this problem by allowing variation at the genetic level and in terms of gene products: that is, we might allow different hard-wired constraints to apply for different languages. But from an evolutionary perspective, proposing constraints which are language-specific and simultaneously innate makes a complete nonsense of the theory. It is also likely to be unworkable, primarily because 84 per cent of the variation found in our species as a whole will occur within any single human population (Barbujani *et al.* 1997), so that it is ludicrously unlikely that a constraint, say FREE-V, would arise only in the group speaking Lardil, and nowhere else. For a start, all speakers of this language would need a common ancestor with the relevant mutation. This might, given small groups, population movements and a lively imagination, just about allow for constraint-based linguistic innovations at the point when language groups diverge; but changes taking place within a single language or variety would present more of a challenge. Furthermore, if we need to consider carefully whether language could reasonably have evolved in upwards of 50,000 years, there seems very little chance of the 'no initial [kn]' constraint proposed by Green (1998), for instance, being reflected innately for English speakers after only a relatively few generations.

OT is, then, on the horns of a dilemma. If all constraints are innate and universal, and therefore available for reranking to account for changes in any language, then natural selection cannot be invoked in the evolution of phonology, and we are faced with the prospect of accounting for the development of a complex, adaptive system without the single mechanism dedicated to just such developments. If, on the other hand, we allow for the introduction of variation in the shape of novel constraints, we must assume that these arise randomly, with a concentration sufficient to allow a general change in Scots Gaelic, or Tagalog, and only there, being almost beyond the bounds of possibility. Even if we allow language-particular constraints to be introduced into the innate constraint system on the basis of novel speaker behaviour, we are effectively countenancing a Lamarckian theory.

Dennett (1995: 321) defines Lamarckism as 'inheritance of acquired characteristics *through the genetic apparatus*'. Lamarck attempted to explain the giraffe's long neck by suggesting that each individual organism stretched its neck muscles throughout its life to reach the foliage on high trees; baby giraffes were then born with longer necks. The neo-Darwinian approach instead proposes that giraffes who happen to be born with longer necks anyway will be favoured reproductively, and therefore that long necks will become more common in the giraffe population; furthermore, natural selection will make them longer across the generations. This might seem intuitively less satisfactory, since the account relies on random mutation to get it going, rather than resting on purpose and intention; but it also incorporates the limitation that only what starts genetic, stays genetic: modified behaviours do not make their way back into the genes.

Lamarck's ideas are extremely unlikely in the absence of evidence, but they are not *a priori* impossible: as Dawkins (1986: 292) says, 'just as somebody may one day see a fairy at the bottom of the garden when sober and in possession of a camera, somebody may one day prove that acquired characteristics can be inherited.' Dawkins also tells us why this is so unlikely, by his further assumption that the genetic code is more like a recipe than a blueprint. Blueprints are in one-to-one correspondence with the buildings they describe, albeit smaller and in fewer dimensions. Bake a cake, however, and there is no single part which corresponds directly to the first word, step or ingredient; but there are one-to-one mappings of differences, in that substituting yeast for baking powder will produce a different result, so that we can still talk about the gene for blue eyes or the gene for muscular dystrophy, for example. It follows that acquired characteristics of a house will be reflected directly in the blueprint; an internal wall knocked down will lead to a line rubbed out on the blueprint. In consequence (Dawkins 1986: 297–8),

if the genes were a blueprint, it would be easy to imagine any characteristic that a body acquired during its lifetime being faithfully transcribed back into the genetic code, and hence passed into the next generation … It is because the genes are not a blueprint but a recipe that this is not possible. We can no more imagine acquired characteristics being inherited than we can imagine the following. A cake has one slice cut out of it. A description of the alteration is now fed back into the recipe, and the recipe changes in such a way that the next cake baked according [to] the altered recipe comes out of the oven with one slice already neatly missing.

It seems that, if we allow unique constraints for particular languages, and if those are introduced into the innate constraint system on the basis of novel speaker behaviour, we are countenancing just such inheritance of acquired characteristics. One possible way around this would be to invoke the so-called 'Baldwin Effect', better known within genetics as genetic assimilation, which derives apparently Lamarckian results from mechanisms reconcilable with Darwinism. Baldwin (1896: 447) argues that his principle of Organic Selection 'secures by survival certain lines of determinate phylogenetic variation in the direction of the determinate ontogenetic adaptations of the earlier generation.' That is to say, if some useful behaviour is partly but not wholly genetically determined, individuals in a species have the capacity to learn the remainder, and the behaviour aids survival; then subsequent generations are likely progressively to learn less and less, with more and more aspects of the trait being gradually incorporated in the genes, leading ultimately to total genetic assimilation. Such arguments have been given, for instance, for fixed-action responses such as mating displays, which began as simply behaviours, but are now genetically determined, since sibling species will have different displays, and hybrids something in between (see Lorenz 1953 on ducks). Adaptive fast learning thus has, as its limiting case, no learning at all. Language is clearly partly learned, and if we accept that it is also selectively advantageous, it might seem a good candidate for genetic assimilation, which might then offer a means of allowing language-specific developments to become genetically encoded. However, the Baldwin Effect relies absolutely on constancy of the environment, and furthermore on an appropriate mutation happening along to be recruited. This could take some time (in the order of hundreds, or even thousands of generations) so that it might well have been a factor in the initial evolution of the language faculty, but is far less likely to play a part in the geneticization of individual traits of individual languages. It follows that the relevance of genetic assimilation to the constraints of OT, if these are indeed simultaneously language-specific and innate, is dubious, and remains to be established, perhaps in part by further simulation experiments (see Briscoe forthcoming). It might be argued that I am setting up a straw man here, since most linguists would deny the possibility of a language-specific trait being innate at all: but given the number of constraints reviewed in earlier chapters which clearly do have language-specific effects, and the strong claims of innateness simultaneously espoused by many of their inventors, the straw man seems to have more life in him than one might suppose.

It would appear that, although we can formulate a general theory of evolution of complex systems by natural selection, and although this can be extended profitably to language, the decisions made by proponents of OT leave the constraints between a rock and a hard place as regards evolution. If we allow unique constraints for particular languages, and if those are introduced into the innate constraint system on the basis of novel speaker behaviour, we are countenancing inheritance of acquired characteristics. The obvious response to this difficulty, namely the argument that there is no such thing as a new constraint, takes us straight back to the problematic picture of the constraints as a fixed set (of apparently infinite size, within a brain of presumably limited capacity): in that case, we return both to saltation, and to the problem of justifying a constraint as universal when its effects are very particular.

It follows from the discussion above that phonologists are now faced with a choice. On the one hand, we could maintain the position of orthodox Optimality Theory and propose a potentially extremely large set of constraints, and an innate system which fits uneasily with much current evolutionary thinking. On the other hand, we could choose to learn from cognate disciplines that there is a place for the particular as well as the universal, and hence for rules, or at least language-specific and learned constraints as well as innate ones. In modern phonology, it often seems that features which cannot somehow be seen as universal are not worthy of our attention. In biology, there is a different approach: Gould (1991: 171) suggests that, although it is important to look for laws and generalizations, there is also a time and a place to 'celebrate diversity and revel in the peculiarities of animals'. And in animals, as in languages, we face the conclusion that things *could* be otherwise: we must describe them as they are; explain them when we can; and try to develop a nose for the difference.

6

Optimality and Optimism: the Panglossian Paradigm

Prince and Smolensky (1993) quote Voltaire as an epigraph: ' "It is demonstrated," he said, "that things cannot be otherwise: for, since everything was made for a purpose, everything is necessarily made for the best purpose" ' (Voltaire, *Candide, or Optimism*: Ch.1). Much of the argument in earlier chapters has tended towards the conclusion that things could almost always be otherwise. It is true that certain observations in biology do follow as a natural consequence of the inviolable laws of physics, and similarly in phonology, certain truly universal facts may reflect inviolable and immutable constraints. For the most part, however, the properties of language or of organisms in general could have evolved differently; and their current configuration, being in part determined by sheer historical accident, could certainly be other than it is. Constraints hypothesized by the theorist to circumscribe only the variation currently attested are therefore themselves shaped by contingency; and we require, in addition, tools for straightforward description. This may give rise to a view of the world rather less comforting, and less amenable to overall explanation, than the one of Prince and Smolensky's quote. However, if we examine the context of that excerpt further, we shall discover that it reflects neither Candide's view, nor Voltaire's.

The assumption that things cannot be otherwise follows from Leibniz's Principle of Sufficient Reason, 'which holds (rather unsurprisingly) that there must be some logical reason why anything is as it is' (Pearson 1992: xiv). First, we must accept that God's creations are imperfect, since He alone is perfect, and His creations are different from Himself. He could have chosen from an infinite number of possible but imperfect worlds; by the Principle of Sufficient Reason, the world He chose is necessarily the best of all possible worlds. In it, good triumphs, but certain goods will have evils as their corollaries, producing trade-offs of the kind familiar from Optimality Theory. The resulting philosophical framework is known as Leibnizian Optimism.

Candide, according to Pearson (1992: viii–ix), tries Optimism and sentences it to death within the framework of the *conte philosophique*, or philosophical tale. This genre may have predated Voltaire, but:

> whether or not the *conte philosophique* already existed, Voltaire would have had to invent it: for it proved the perfect medium of expression for the sceptic and empiricist that Voltaire was. Deeply suspicious of metaphysics and 'systems', he was constantly appealing to the facts: fiction, paradoxically, allowed him to show the ways in which the muddle and miseries of life could not be reduced to neat, abstract theories.

Voltaire's life in the few years preceding the start of work on *Candide* in 1757 might indeed not be expected to predispose him favourably to the idea that everything was for the best. He fell out of favour at Court; his ex-mistress died in childbirth (and the child wasn't his, either); and he had an acrimonious falling out with Frederick the Great, who had him arrested. The great Lisbon earthquake of 1755, which killed 40,000 people, affected Voltaire profoundly; he could not see either why this should contribute to the greater good, or what Lisbon in particular had done to deserve such a fate. His work on the *Essay on the Manners and Spirits of Nations*, published in 1756, also left him rather depressed about the human condition: 'Given man's inhumanity to man since the dawn of time, he was now even less ready to accept the philosophy of Optimism than before' (Pearson 1992: xx). Although his personal circumstances had improved somewhat by the time he wrote *Candide*, Voltaire still uses his tale to attack savagely 'the belief, which he felt to be characteristic of the rationalism of his age, that logic and reason can somehow explain away the chaotic wretchedness of existence by grandly and metaphysically ignoring the facts' (Pearson 1992: xx).

The framework for *Candide* is provided by the familiar chivalric romance. Candide himself, a young man of uncertain parentage, is brought up in the fabulous castle of Thunder-ten-tronckh, but is kicked out for making advances to the daughter of the house, Cunégonde: 'And all was consternation in the most beautiful and most agreeable of all possible castles' (*Candide*: 3). The rest of the story relates Candide's various attempts to find his beloved, with a running Optimistic commentary supplied by the inimitable Dr Pangloss.

Pangloss, who 'taught metaphysico-theologico-cosmo-codology' to Candide and Cunégonde (*Candide*: 2), is the mouthpiece for Optimism, and a particularly simplistic and all-encompassing version of it, at that. He is absolutely determined that Optimism, and only Optimism, will explain every aspect of the world and man's travails in it, and pursues his philosophy relentlessly to its logical conclusion, without for a moment discerning the lack of logic lurking there. Hence, in context, his contention that things cannot be otherwise becomes ludicrous (*Candide*: 2):

"It is demonstrably true," he would say, "that things cannot be other than as they are. For, everything having been made for a purpose, everything is necessarily made for the best purpose. Observe how noses were made to bear spectacles, and so we have spectacles. Legs are evidently devised to be clad in breeches, and breeches we have. Stones were formed in such a way that they can be hewn and made into castles, and so His Lordship has a very beautiful castle ... "

In similar vein, Pangloss can always find some good to counteract any apparent evil, not noticing that the latter often hugely outweighs the former. Syphilis, for example, is 'an indispensable part of the best of all possible worlds, a necessary ingredient. For if Columbus, on an island in the Americas, had not caught this disease which poisons the spring of procreation, and which is evidently the opposite of what nature intended, we would have neither chocolate nor cochineal' (*Candide*: 9). Pangloss maintains this positive outlook through 'the various atrocities and disasters of which the story provides such a seemingly inexhaustible catalogue. Rape, pillage, murder, massacre, butchery, religious intolerance and abuse, torture, hanging, storm, shipwreck, earthquake, disease, prostitution: all is well' (Pearson 1992: xx). Candide, on the other hand, begins to find it difficult to see the Panglossian point: ' "If this is the best of all possible worlds, then what must the others be like?" ' (*Candide*: 14). He does attempt to stay Optimistic: en route from Spain to Paraguay, ' "We're going to another world," Candide would say. "I expect it must be there that all is well. For you have to admit, one could grumble rather at what goes on in our one" ' (*Candide*: 22). Gradually, however, Candide comes to recognize Pangloss's intransigence for what it is, and on encountering slavery he rejects Optimism altogether, denouncing it as ' "a mania for insisting that all is well when things are going badly" ' (*Candide*: 50). His stance is supported by his meeting with Martin, who nihilistically assumes that the world was created solely for the purpose of driving us mad; but Candide is now thinking for himself, and is wary of accepting this viewpoint wholesale either. In the end, Candide (older and somewhat wiser) is indeed reunited with Cunégonde (older and much uglier); he not only accepts his lot, but finds solace in shaping his ill-assorted band of companions into a self-sufficient little community. Work, Voltaire suggests, is at worst a decent way of distracting our attention from how terrible the world is; at best, it may allow us to take control of our own destiny, and to make real if minor improvements to the world.

Dr Pangloss has already made an appearance in the literature on biological evolution, in Gould and Lewontin's (1979) paper 'The spandrels of San Marco and the Panglossian paradigm'. The paradigm attacked, as we have seen, is the one assuming adaptation as the sole mechanism of evolution; and it is Panglossian in its inflexibility and intransigence: Gould and Lewontin contend that, even when confronted with evidence which seems irreconcilable with a purely adaptationist approach, adaptationists attempt to maintain their position, just as 'Pangloss admitted that he had always suffered horribly; but having once maintained that everything was going marvellously, he still maintained it' (*Candide*: 90). To make real progress, Gould and Lewontin argue, we must rigorously test each proposed adaptationist explanation, and must in general be open to the possibility that alternative or additional mechanisms exist. Sometimes, we will find features which are spandrels, or by-products of some other principle or structure, which may themselves be recruited by natural selection for some future adaptive purpose. In other cases, historical accidents may intervene: as we have seen, an adaptive account of why rhinos have horns might be a reasonable goal, but we would be hard pushed to give a sensible explanation in adaptive terms for the number of horns that arise. Thus, Gould and Lewontin (1979: 581) 'fault the adaptationist programme for its failure to distinguish current utility from reasons for origin', a failing which clearly recapitulates Dr Pangloss's account of noses as having been designed for spectacles or legs for breeches.

Precisely parallel difficulties arise for Optimality Theory, which is in danger of inflexibility in its central contention that constraints will be first, last and always the explanation for phonological behaviour. This is not to deny that violable constraints are appropriate in some cases, but rather to stress that seeing them as all-encompassing means the situations where they do work can be obscured by the situations where they don't. Gould and Lewontin point out that, if the short front legs of *Tyrannosaurus rex* had arisen *de novo*, we might be justified in seeking an adaptive explanation; however, the fact that homologous structures exist in the dinosaur's relatives might suggest instead that the reduction in size is a correlate of some other factor in this particular species, most plausibly walking upright. Similarly, an OT account of the centring diphthongs in modern Southern British English would regard them as arising from the interplay of innate, defeasible constraints. But these vowels did not arise *de novo* either, and their existence owes a good deal to the prior contextually conditioned loss of [r], which in itself may reflect phonetic factors outside phonology altogether. Seeking theory-internal explanation is not enough, in biology or in linguistics; we must be able to appeal to some higher authority outside the field at hand, whether this be the laws of physics for evolutionists, or aspects of phonetics and neurolinguistics for phonologists. Some of these might, indeed, be encoded in OT as inviolable constraints, but so far, no such category of constraints is recognized in the theory.

A substantial problem for both evolutionary theory and OT is that relinquishing a single explanation type in favour of system-specific description for some phenomena can be seen as admitting defeat; it might also acknowledge a lack of ingenuity, since an adaptive or constraint-based account is always possible: 'plausible stories can always be told' (Gould and Lewontin 1979: 588), even if, as we have seen, we might need extra machinery to accommodate them. As Voltaire tells us, however, concocting plausible stories might not always constitute progress. Candide brings back a large red sheep from the lost land of Eldorado where, to indulge in a neo-Darwinian anachronism, geographical isolation has presumably led to a different course of evolution from the common ancestor shared with our sheep. Unable to take the sheep on his journeys, he rather sadly leaves it at the Academy of Science at Bordeaux, the members of which 'set as the subject of that year's prize the question why the wool of this sheep was red, and the prize was awarded to a scientist from the North who proved by A plus B minus C divided by Z that the sheep has necessarily to be red, and to die of sheep-pox' (*Candide*: 58). This scientist might be greatly feted by his colleagues; but his proof does not deal with the fact that the circumstances of life are just different in Eldorado and in France. Things can be otherwise, and often are. Sometimes it is necessary to accept that; and to accept description, and partial historical explanation without possibility of prediction, as the best we can do, and indeed the best we will ever be able to do. As I have already suggested, phonology may in fact be at an advantage here over such cognate disciplines as biological evolution, in having at its disposal two types of formal mechanism, constraints and rules, to deal with universal, though variable, and specific behaviour respectively. What OT is asking us to do is to throw one of these away.

What, then, is the future for Optimality Theory? In the light of the discussion above, the first and most important task for the model must be a full assessment of the universality of constraints: are absolutely universal and inviolable constraints required in addition to the rankable and defeasible ones; and, of the latter class, are some in fact language-particular? Any assessment of whether Universal Grammar as envisaged in OT constitutes a system evolvable by natural selection will depend on our answers to these questions. If language-particular constraints are rejected in favour of system-specific rules, then the interaction between rules and constraints will have to be investigated and clarified, as will novel types of constraints and additional machinery such as Output–Output constraints, Sympathy, and level-ordering within OT; this will also have immediate and serious consequences for the acquisition of OT, and the treatment of sound change in the theory. Finally, the apparent superiority of OT over derivational models on the grounds that the former contains only constraints while the latter involve rules and constraints can no longer be maintained, and instead a comparison between a model with rules plus constraints on well-formedness versus one with rules plus constraints on rule applications will become a priority. Archangeli (1997: 15 fn.3) points out that '... there are numerous analyses involving constraints whose status as a universal is minimal at best. At this point, it is unclear whether this is a weakness of the model itself, or a weakness of the analysis.' On the contrary, my claim is that this is not a weakness at all, so long as we identify these system-specific constraints or rules as a different set of descriptors, and crucially as non-innate. Recognizing that there really are language-specific aspects of phonology is simply facing facts, accepting the obvious, recognizing the way the world is, whatever you want to call it. A phonology with rules and constraints, as we have seen, is simply allying itself with all kinds of other models concerned with the dynamics of complex systems, in recognizing that some phenomena are universal and predictable, although they may vary in a limited way across systems, while others are truly system-specific and contingent.

In short, there is a great deal of work to do, and it will not be done by inflexibly attempting to fit every phonological phenomenon into a constraint-based theory, where all constraints are universal, violable and innate, at all costs, but by considering a wide range of synchronic and diachronic data and confronting their implications for the model. Candide, at the end of his travels, has realized that the consolations of an intransigent philosophy may be vastly out of proportion to the time and trouble spent arriving at them, whereas dealing with life methodically, issue by issue, is the only way to make progress; he deserves the last word (*Candide*: 92–3):

And sometimes Pangloss would say to Candide:
"All events form a chain in the best of all possible worlds. For in the end, if you had not been given a good kick up the backside and chased out of a beautiful castle for loving Miss Cunégonde, and if you hadn't been subjected to the Inquisition, and if you hadn't wandered about America on foot, and if you hadn't dealt the Baron a good blow with your sword, and if you hadn't lost all your sheep from that fine country of Eldorado, you wouldn't be here now eating candied citron and pistachio nuts."

"That is well put," replied Candide, "but we must cultivate our garden."

References

ALDRIDGE, Susan (1996). *The Thread of Life: the story of genes and genetic engineering*. Cambridge: Cambridge University Press.

ANTTILA, Arto (1997). 'Deriving variation from grammar', in Frans Hinskens, Roeland van der Hout, and W. Leo Wetzels (eds.), *Variation, Change and Phonological Theory*. Amsterdam: Benjamins, 35–68.

——and Young-mee Yu CHO (1998). 'Variation and change in Optimality Theory'. *Lingua*, **104**: 31–56.

ARCHANGELI, Diana (1988). 'Aspects of underspecification theory'. *Phonology*, **5**: 183–207.

——(1997). 'Optimality Theory: An introduction to linguistics in the 1990s', in Diana Archangeli and D. Terence Langendoen (eds.), *Optimality Theory: An Overview*. Oxford: Blackwell, 1–32.

——and D. Terence LANGENDOEN (eds.) (1997*a*). *Optimality Theory: An Overview*. Oxford: Blackwell.

——(1997*b*). 'Afterword', in Diana Archangeli and D. Terence Langendoen (eds.), *Optimality Theory: An Overview*. Oxford: Blackwell, 200–15.

——and Keiichiro SUZUKI (1997). 'The Yokuts challenge', in Iggy Roca (ed.), *Derivations and Constraints in Phonology*. Oxford: Clarendon Press, 197–226.

BALDWIN, J. Mark (1896). 'A new factor in evolution'. *The American Naturalist*, **XXX**: 441–51.

BARBUJANI, Guido, Arianna MAGAGNI, Eric MINCH, and L. L. CAVALLI-SFORZA (1997). 'An apportionment of human DNA diversity'. *Proceedings of the National Academy of Sciences of the USA*, **94**: 4516–19.

BATALI, John (1998). 'Computational simulations of the emergence of grammar', in James R. Hurford, Michael Studdert-Kennedy, and Chris Knight (eds.), *Approaches to the Evolution of Language*. Cambridge: Cambridge University Press, 405–26.

BENUA, Laura (1995). 'Identity effects in morphological truncation', in Jill Beckman, Laura Walsh Dickey, and Suzanne Urbanczyk (eds.), *Papers in Optimality Theory*. University of Massachusetts Occasional Papers in Linguistics, **18**. Amherst, MA: Graduate Linguistic Student Association, 77–136.

BENUA, Laura (1997). *Transderivational Identity: Phonological relations between words.* Unpublished PhD Dissertation, University of Massachusetts at Amherst.

BERMÚDEZ-OTERO, Ricardo (1999). *Constraint Interaction in Language Change: Quantity in English and German.* Unpublished PhD Dissertation, Department of English and American Studies, University of Manchester.

BICKERTON, Derek (1991). 'Language origins and evolutionary plausibility'. *Language and Cognition,* 11.

BLEVINS, Juliette (1997). 'Rules in Optimality Theory: two case studies', in Iggy Roca (ed.), *Derivations and Constraints in Phonology.* Oxford: Clarendon Press, 227–60.

—— and Andrew GARRETT (1998). 'The origins of consonant–vowel metathesis.' Ms, to appear in *Language.*

BRISCOE, Ted (forthcoming). 'Language Acquisition: The Bioprogram Hypothesis and the Baldwin Effect'. To appear in *Language.*

BROADBENT, Judith (1991). 'Linking and intrusive r in English'. *University College London Working Papers in Linguistics,* 3: 281–302.

Candide and Other Stories, Voltaire (1757). Ed. Roger Pearson (1992) London, Everyman's Library.

CARSTAIRS-McCARTHY, Andrew (1999). *The Origins of Complex Language: An enquiry into the evolutionary beginnings of sentences, syllables, and truth.* Oxford: Oxford University Press.

CHEN, M. (1987). 'The syntax of Xiamen tone sandhi'. *Phonology Yearbook,* 4: 109–49.

CHO, Young-mee Yu (1995). 'Language change as reranking of constraints'. Paper presented at the 12th International Conference on Historical Linguistics, University of Manchester.

CHOMSKY, Noam (1975). *Reflections on Language.* New York: Pantheon.

—— (1982). *The Generative Enterprise: A discussion with Riny Huybregts and Henk van Riemsdijk.* Dordrecht: Foris.

—— (1988). *Language and Problems of Knowledge: the Managua Lectures.* Cambridge, MA: MIT Press.

—— (1991). 'Linguistics and cognitive science: problems and mysteries', in Asa Kasher (ed.), *The Chomskyan Turn: Generative Linguistics, Philosophy, Mathematics, and Psychology.* Oxford: Blackwell, 26–55.

—— and Morris HALLE (1968). *The Sound Pattern of English.* New York: Harper & Row.

CRONIN, Helena (1991). *The Ant and the Peacock*. Cambridge: Cambridge University Press.

DARWIN, Charles (1859). *The Origin of Species*. London: John Murray. Reprinted 1996. Oxford: Oxford University Press World's Classics.

DAWKINS, Richard (1986). *The Blind Watchmaker*. London: Penguin.

—— (1995). *River out of Eden*. London: Phoenix.

DEACON, Terrence (1997). *The Symbolic Species*. London: Penguin.

DENNETT, Daniel C. (1995). *Darwin's Dangerous Idea*. London: Allen Lane.

DONEGAN, Patricia (1993). 'On the phonetic basis of phonological change', in Charles Jones (ed.), *Historical Linguistics: Problems and Perspectives*. London: Longman, 98–130.

DRESSLER, Wolfgang U. (1985). 'On the predictiveness of Natural Morphology'. *Journal of Linguistics*, 21: 321–37.

—— Willi MAYERTHALER, Oswald PANAGL, and Wolfgang U. WURZEL (1987). *Leitmotifs in Natural Morphology*. Amsterdam: Benjamins.

DUNBAR, Robin (1996). *Grooming, Gossip and the Evolution of Language*. London: Faber & Faber.

—— (1998). 'Theory of mind and the evolution of language', in James R. Hurford, Michael Studdert-Kennedy, and Chris Knight (eds.), *Approaches to the Evolution of Language*. Cambridge: Cambridge University Press, 92–110.

FAARLUND, Jan Terje (1990). *Syntactic Change: Towards a Theory of Historical Syntax*. Berlin: Mouton de Gruyter.

FELSENSTEIN, J. (1989). 'PHYLIP—phylogeny inference package (Version 3.2.)'. *Cladistics*, 5: 164–6.

FISHER, R. A. (1930). *The Genetical Theory of Natural Selection*. Oxford: Oxford University Press.

FLEMMING, Edward S. (1996). 'Laryngeal metathesis in Cherokee', in Pamela Munro (ed.), *Cherokee Papers from UCLA*. UCLA Occasional Papers in Linguistics, 16. Los Angeles: Department of Linguistics, UCLA, 23–44.

GIEGERICH, Heinz J. (1999). *Lexical Strata in English: Morphological causes, phonological effects*. Cambridge: Cambridge University Press.

GOULD, Stephen Jay (1991). *Ever Since Darwin*. London: Penguin.

—— and R. C. LEWONTIN (1979). 'The spandrels of San Marco and the Panglossian paradigm: a critique of the adaptionist programme'. *Proceedings of the Royal Society of London, Series B*, 205: 581–98.

GREEN, Antony Dubach (1998). 'The promotion of the unmarked: representing sound change in Optimality Theory'. Paper presented at the 10th International Conference on English Historical Linguistics, University of Manchester.

GREENBERG, Joseph H. (1963). 'Some universals of language with particular reference to the order of meaningful elements', in Joseph H. Greenberg (ed.), *Universals of Language.* Cambridge, MA: MIT Press, 73–113.

GRIMSHAW, Jane (1997). 'Projection, heads, and optimality'. *Linguistic Inquiry,* **28**: 373–422.

GUY, Gregory R. (1997*a*). 'Violable is variable: Optimality Theory and linguistic variation'. *Language Variation and Change,* **9**: 333–47.

—— (1997*b*). 'Competence, performance, and the generative grammar of variation', in Frans Hinskens, Roeland van der Hout, and W. Leo Wetzels (eds.), *Variation, Change and Phonological Theory.* Amsterdam: Benjamins, 125–43.

HALE, Mark, and Charles REISS (1998). 'Formal and empirical arguments concerning phonological acquisition'. *Linguistic Inquiry,* **29**: 656–83.

HALLE, Morris, and William J. IDSARDI (1997). '*r*, hypercorrection, and the Elsewhere Condition', in Iggy Roca (ed.), *Derivations and Constraints in Phonology.* Oxford: Clarendon Press, 331–48.

HARGUS, Sharon, and Ellen M. KAISSE (eds.) (1993). *Studies in Lexical Phonology.* New York: Academic Press.

HARRIS, Alice, and Lyle CAMPBELL (1995). *Historical Syntax in Cross-Linguistic Perspective.* Cambridge: Cambridge University Press.

HARRIS, John (1989). 'Towards a lexical analysis of sound change in progress'. *Journal of Linguistics,* **25**: 35–56.

HASPELMATH, Martin (1999). 'Optimality and diachronic adaptation'. Ms; to appear in *Zeitschrift für Sprachwissenschaft.*

HAWKINS, John A. (1994). *A Performance Theory of Order and Constituency.* Cambridge: Cambridge University Press.

HAYES, Bruce P. (1996). 'Phonetically-driven phonology: the role of Optimality Theory and inductive grounding'. Ms, Rutgers Optimality Archive.

HINSKENS, Frans, Roeland VAN DER HOUT, and W. Leo WETZELS (eds.) (1997). *Variation, Change and Phonological Theory.* Amsterdam: Benjamins.

HUME, Elizabeth V. (1997). 'Vowel preservation in Leti'. *Oceanic Linguistics,* **36**: 65–101.

HURFORD, James R. (1992). 'An approach to the phylogeny of the language faculty', in John A. Hawkins and Murray Gell-Mann (eds.), *The Evolution of Human Languages*. Reading, MA: Addison-Wesley, 273–303.

—— Michael STUDDERT-KENNEDY, and Chris KNIGHT (eds.) (1998). *Approaches to the Evolution of Language*. Cambridge: Cambridge University Press.

HUTTON, John (1996). 'Optimality Theory and historical language change'. Paper presented at the Manchester Phonology Workshop.

JAEGER, Jeri J. (1986). 'On the acquisition of abstract representations for English vowels'. *Phonology Yearbook*, 3: 71–97.

JERISON, Harry J. (1973). *The Evolution of the Brain and Intelligence*. New York: Academic Press.

KAGER, René (1999). *Optimality Theory*. Cambridge: Cambridge University Press.

KENSTOWICZ, Michael, and Charles KISSEBERTH (1979). *Generative Phonology: Description and Theory*. New York: Academic Press.

KIPARSKY, Paul (1982). 'Lexical phonology and morphology', in I.-S. Yang (ed.), *Linguistics in the Morning Calm*. Seoul: Hanshin, 3–91.

KIRBY, Simon (1998). 'Fitness and the selective adaptation of language', in James R. Hurford, Michael Studdert-Kennedy, and Chris Knight (eds.), *Approaches to the Evolution of Language*. Cambridge: Cambridge University Press, 359–83.

—— (1999). *Function, Selection, and Innateness: The emergence of language universals*. Oxford: Oxford University Press.

KIRCHNER, Robert (1996). 'Synchronic chain shifts in Optimality Theory'. *Linguistic Inquiry*, 27: 341–50.

—— (1997). 'Contrastiveness and faithfulness'. *Phonology*, **14**: 83–111.

KLEIN, Thomas (1997). 'Output constraints and prosodic correspondence in Chamorro reduplication'. *Linguistic Inquiry*, **28**: 707–15.

KUNO, Susumo (1974). 'The position of relative clauses and conjunctions'. *Linguistic Inquiry*, 5: 117–36.

LABOV, William (1972). *Sociolinguistic Patterns*. Philadelphia: University of Pennsylvania Press.

—— (1994). *Principles of Linguistic Change. Vol. 1: Internal Factors*. Oxford: Blackwell.

LASS, Roger (1980). *On Explaining Language Change*. Cambridge: Cambridge University Press.

LASS, Roger (1990). 'How to do things with junk: exaptation in language evolution'. *Journal of Linguistics,* 26: 79–102.

—— (1997). *Historical Linguistics and Language Change.* Cambridge: Cambridge University Press.

LEHMANN, Winfred P. (1973). 'A structural principle of language and its implications'. *Language,* 49: 47–66.

LIGHTFOOT, David (1979). *Principles of Diachronic Syntax.* Cambridge: Cambridge University Press.

—— (1981). 'A reply to some critics'. *Lingua,* 55: 351–68.

—— (1991a). *How to Set Parameters: Arguments from Language Change.* Cambridge, MA: MIT Press.

—— (1991b). 'Subjacency and sex'. *Language and Communication,* 11.

—— (1999). *The Development of Language: Acquisition, Change, and Evolution.* Oxford: Blackwell.

LIN, Yen-Hwei (1997). 'Syllabic and moraic structures in Piro'. *Phonology,* 14: 403–36.

LORENZ, Konrad (1953). 'Comparative studies on the behaviour of the Anatinae'. *Aviculture Magazine*: 1–87.

MADDIESON, Ian (1984). *Patterns of Sounds.* Cambridge: Cambridge University Press.

MARCUS, G. F. (1993). 'Negative evidence in language acquisition'. *Cognition,* 46: 53–85.

MATTHEWS, Peter (1981). *Do languages obey general laws?* Inaugural lecture, University of Cambridge. Cambridge: Cambridge University Press.

MAYERTHALER, W. (1988). Naturalness in Morphology. Ann Arbor: Karoma.

McCARTHY, John (1991). 'Synchronic rule inversion', in L. A. Sutton, C. Johnson, and R. Shields (eds.), *Proceedings of the 17th Annual Meeting of the Berkeley Linguistics Society.* Berkeley, CA: Berkeley Linguistics Society, 192–207.

—— (1993). 'A case of surface constraint violation'. *Canadian Journal of Linguistics,* 38: 169–95.

—— (1998a). 'Sympathy and phonological opacity'. Ms, Rutgers Optimality Archive.

—— (1998b). 'Sympathy, cumulativity, and the Duke-of-York gambit'. Ms, Rutgers Optimality Archive.

—— (1999). 'Optimality Theory: Its goals and key assumptions'. Paper presented at the Linguistics Association of Great Britain Spring Meeting, University of Manchester.

McCarthy, John, and Alan S. Prince (1995). 'Faithfulness and reduplicative identity', in Jill Beckman, Laura Walsh Dickey, and Suzanne Urbanczyk (eds.), *Papers in Optimality Theory*. University of Massachusetts Occasional Papers in Linguistics, **18**. Amherst, MA: Graduate Linguistic Student Association, 249–384.

McMahon, April (1990). 'Vowel shift, free rides and strict cyclicity'. *Lingua*, 80: 197–225.

—— (1991). 'Lexical Phonology and sound change: the case of the Scottish Vowel Length Rule'. *Journal of Linguistics*, 27: 29–53.

—— (1994). *Understanding Language Change*. Cambridge: Cambridge University Press.

—— (1996). 'On the use of the past to explain the present: the history of /r/ in English and Scots', in Derek Britton (ed.), *English Historical Linguistics 1994*. Amsterdam: Benjamins, 73–89.

—— (2000). *Lexical Phonology and the History of English*. Cambridge: Cambridge University Press.

—— Paul Foulkes, and Laura Tollfree (1994). 'Gestural representation and Lexical Phonology'. *Phonology*, 11: 277–316.

Merchant, Jason (1996). 'Alignment and fricative assimilation in German'. *Linguistic Inquiry*, 27: 709–19.

Miglio, Viola (1998). 'The Great Vowel Shift: An OT model for unconditioned language change'. Paper presented at the 10th International Conference on English Historical Linguistics, University of Manchester.

Milroy, James (1992). *Linguistic Variation and Change*. Oxford: Blackwell.

Mohanan, K. P. (1986). *The Theory of Lexical Phonology*. Dordrecht: Reidel.

Morell, Virginia (1997). 'Fossilized hatchling heats up the bird–dinosaur debate'. *Science*, 276: 1501.

Nagy, Naomi and Bill Reynolds (1997). 'Optimality Theory and variable word-final deletion in Faetar'. *Language Variation and Change*, 9: 37–55.

Nettle, Daniel (1999a). *Linguistic Diversity*. Oxford: Oxford University Press.

—— (1999b). 'Using Social Impact Theory to simulate language change'. *Lingua*, 108: 95–117.

—— (1999c). 'Is the rate of linguistic change constant?' *Lingua*, 108: 119–36.

Newmeyer, Frederick J. (1991). 'Functional explanation in linguistics and the origins of language'. *Language and Communication*, 11: 3–99.

NEWMEYER, Frederick J. (1998*a*). 'On the supposed "counterfunction-ality" of Universal Grammar: some evolutionary implications', in James R. Hurford, Michael Studdert-Kennedy, and Chris Knight (eds.), *Approaches to the Evolution of Language*. Cambridge: Cambridge University Press, 305–19.

—— (1998*b*). 'The irrelevance of typology to grammatical theory'. Paper presented at the Linguistics Association of Great Britain Spring Meeting, University of Lancaster.

NILSSON, Dan-E., and Susanne PELGER (1994). 'A pessimistic estimate of the time required for an eye to evolve'. *Proceedings of the Royal Society of London, Series B*, **256**: 53–8. Reprinted in Mark Ridley (ed.) (1997), *Evolution*. Oxford: Oxford University Press, 293–301.

OHALA, John (1981). 'The listener as a source of sound change', in Carrie S. Masek, Roberta A. Hendrick, and Mary Frances Miller (eds.) (1997), *Papers from the Parasession on Language and Behavior*. Chicago: Chicago Linguistic Society, 178–203.

ORGUN, C. Orhan (1996). *Sign-Based Morphology and Phonology: with special attention to Optimality Theory*. Unpublished PhD Dissertation, University of California at Berkeley.

PARADIS, Carole, and Darlene LACHARITÉ (1993). 'Introduction to special issue on Constraint-Based Theories in Multilinear Phonology'. *Canadian Journal of Linguistics*, **38**: 127–53.

PEARSON, Roger (1992). 'Introduction'. *Candide and Other Stories*. Voltaire. London: Everyman's Library, vii–lviii.

PESETSKY, David (1997). 'Optimality Theory and Syntax: Movement and pronunciation', in Diana Archangeli and D. Terence Langendoen (eds.), *Optimality Theory: An Overview*. Oxford: Blackwell, 134–70.

PIATTELLI-PALMARINI, Massimo (1989). 'Evolution, selection and cogni-tion: from "learning" to parameter setting in biology and in the study of language'. *Cognition*, **31**: 1–44.

PILBEAM, David, and Stephen Jay GOULD (1974). 'Size and scaling in human evolution'. *Science*, **186**: 892–901.

PINKER, Steven (1994). *The Language Instinct*. London: Penguin.

—— (1997). 'Evolutionary biology and the evolution of language', in Myrna Gopnik (ed.), *The Inheritance and Innateness of Grammars*. Oxford: Oxford University Press, 181–208.

—— and Paul BLOOM (1990). 'Natural language and natural selection'. *Behavioral and Brain Sciences*, **13**: 707–84.

POWER, Camilla (1998). 'Old wives' tales: the gossip hypothesis and the reliability of cheap signals', in James R. Hurford, Michael Studdert-Kennedy, and Chris Knight (eds.), *Approaches to the Evolution of Language*. Cambridge: Cambridge University Press, 111–29.

PREMACK, David (1985). ' "Gavagai!" or the future history of the animal language controversy'. *Cognition*, 19: 207–96.

PRINCE, Alan, and Paul SMOLENSKY (1993). *Optimality Theory: Constraint Interaction in Generative Grammar*. Manuscript, Rutgers University/University of Colorado at Boulder.

PULLEYBLANK, Douglas (1997). 'Optimality Theory and features', in Diana Archangeli and D. Terence Langendoen (eds.), *Optimality Theory: An Overview*. Oxford: Blackwell, 59–101.

—— and William J. TURKEL (1997). 'Gradient retreat', in Iggy Roca (ed.), *Derivations and Constraints in Phonology*. Oxford: Clarendon Press, 153–93.

RIDLEY, Matt (1999). *Genome: The autobiography of a species in 23 chapters*. London: Fourth Estate.

RINGEN, Catherine O., and Robert M. VAGO (1998). 'Hungarian vowel harmony in Optimality Theory'. *Phonology*, 15: 393–416.

ROCA, Iggy (1997). 'Derivations or constraints, or derivations and constraints?', in Iggy Roca (ed.), *Derivations and Constraints in Phonology*. Oxford: Clarendon Press, 3–41.

ROMAINE, Suzanne (1981). 'The transparency principle: what it is and why it doesn't work'. *Lingua*, 55: 277–300.

ROSE, Sharon (1997). 'Featural morphology and dialect variation: the contribution of historical change', in Frans Hinskens, Roeland van der Hout, and W. Leo Wetzels (eds.), *Variation, Change and Phonological Theory*. Amsterdam: Benjamins, 231–66.

RUSSELL, Kevin (1997). 'Optimality Theory and Morphology', in Diana Archangeli and D. Terence Langendoen (eds.), *Optimality Theory: An Overview*. Oxford: Blackwell, 102–33.

SCHLINDWEIN SCHMIDT, Deborah (1996). 'Vowel raising in Basaa.' *Phonology*, 13: 239–67.

SCHMIDT-NIELSEN, Knut (1972). *How Animals Work*. Cambridge: Cambridge University Press.

SHERRARD, Nicholas (1997). 'Questions of priorities: an introductory overview of Optimality Theory in phonology', in Iggy Roca (ed.), *Derivations and Constraints in Phonology*. Oxford: Clarendon Press, 43–89.

SMITH, N. V. (1981). 'Consistency, markedness and language change: on the notion "consistent language" '. *Journal of Linguistics*, 17: 39–54.

SOBER, Elliott (1990). 'Comment on Pinker and Bloom'. *Behavioral and Brain Sciences*, 13: 764.

SPEAS, Margaret (1997). 'Optimality Theory and Syntax: Null pronouns and control', in Diana Archangeli and D. Terence Langendoen (eds.), *Optimality Theory: An Overview*. Oxford: Blackwell, 171–99.

STAMPE, David (1972). *How I Spent My Summer Vacation*. Unpublished PhD Dissertation, Department of Linguistics, Ohio State University.

STERIADE, Donca (1995). 'Positional neutralization'. Ms, Rutgers Optimality Archive.

SWOFFORD, D. L. (1990). *PAUP: Phylogenetic Analysis Using Parsimony. Computer program*. Washington DC: Laboratory of Molecular Systematics, National Museum of Natural History, Smithsonian Institution.

TESAR, Bruce, and Paul SMOLENSKY (1998). 'Learnability in Optimality Theory'. *Linguistic Inquiry*, 29: 229–68.

THOMPSON, D'Arcy W. (1917). *On Growth and Form*. Cambridge: Cambridge University Press.

VENNEMANN, Theo (1972). 'Rule inversion'. *Lingua*, 29: 209–42.

—— (1974). 'Topics, subjects and word order: from SXV to SVX via TVX', in John M. Anderson and Charles Jones (eds.), *Historical Linguistics. Volume 1*. Amsterdam: North Holland, 339–76.

VINCENT, Nigel (1976). 'Perceptual factors and word order change in Latin', in Martin Harris (ed.), *Romance Syntax*. Salford: University of Salford Press, 54–68.

WANG, H. Samuel, and Bruce DERWING (1986). 'More on English vowel shift: the back vowel question'. *Phonology Yearbook*, 3: 99–116.

WEST, Geoffrey B., James H. BROWN, and Brian J. ENQUIST (1997). 'A general model for the origin of allometric scaling laws in biology'. *Science*, 276: 122–6.

WILLIAMS, George (1985). 'A defence of reductionism in evolutionary biology'. *Oxford Surveys in Evolutionary Biology*, 2: 1–27.

WURZEL, Wolfgang U. (1989). *Inflectional Morphology and Naturalness*. Dordrecht: Kluwer.

ZUBRITSKAYA, Katya (1997). 'Mechanism of sound change in Optimality Theory'. *Language Variation and Change*, 9: 121–48.

Index

Note: The names of particular constraints are listed under 'constraints – individual'. Page numbers in bold type indicate the location where a constraint is defined or formally stated.